UNSTRESS YOUR LIFE

THE NO NONSENSE LIBRARY

NO NONSENSE HEALTH GUIDES

Women's Health and Fitness
A Diet for Lifetime Health
A Guide to Exercise and Fitness Equipment
How to Tone and Trim Your Trouble Spots
Stretch for Health
Unstress Your Life
Calories, Carbohydrates and Sodium

NO NONSENSE FINANCIAL GUIDES

NO NONSENSE REAL ESTATE GUIDES

NO NONSENSE LEGAL GUIDES

NO NONSENSE CAREER GUIDES

NO NONSENSE SUCCESS GUIDES

NO NONSENSE COOKING GUIDES

NO NONSENSE WINE GUIDES

NO NONSENSE PARENTING GUIDES

UNSTRESS YOUR LIFE

How to Reduce Tension and Feel Great

By the Editors of
Prevention® Magazine

Longmeadow Press

Notice

This book is intended as a reference volume only, not as a medical manual or guide to self-treatment. It is not intended as a substitute for the medical advice of physicians. The reader should regularly consult a physician in general, and particularly for any symptoms. If you suspect that you have a medical problem, we urge you to seek competent medical help. Keep in mind that exercise and nutritional needs vary from person to person, depending on age, sex, health status and individual variations. The information here is intended to help you make informative decisions about your health, not as a substitute for any treatment that may have been prescribed by your doctor.

Unstress Your Life

Copyright © 1987 Rodale Press, Inc. All Rights Reserved.

Cover Art © 1987 by Rodale Press

Published April 1987 for Longmeadow Press, 201 High Ridge Road, Stamford, CT 06904. No part of this book may be reproduced or used in any form or by any means, electronic or mechanical, including photocopying, recording, or by any information storage and retrieval system, without permission in writing from the publisher.

Library of Congress Cataloging-in-Publication Data

Unstress your life.

    (No-nonsense health guide)
    1. Stress (Psychology)—Prevention. 2. Adjustment (Psychology)
I. Prevention (Emmaus, Pa.) II. Series. [DNLM: 1. Disease—etiology—
popular works. 2. Stress, Psychological—popular works. WM 172 U59]
BF575.S75U57   1987   155.9   87-4150
ISBN 0-681-40135-4   paperback

Special thanks to Jeff Meade for compiling and editing the information in this book.

Book design by Acey Lee and Lisa Gatti

Illustrations by Susan Rosenberger

No Nonsense Health Guide is a trademark controlled by Longmeadow Press.

2   4   6   8   10   9   7   5   3   paperback

Contents

The Mind-Body Connection

Whether you're trapped in a traffic jam or have just won a bet on the Indy 500; whether you're quarreling with someone or have just been given a surprise kiss; whether a stressful situation is painful or pleasurable—the interior physiological drama is the same. In simplified form, here's what happens: A portion of the brain—the hypothalamus—perceives the stressful event and immediately triggers an "alarm reaction." Electrochemical messengers race to various parts of the body, mobilizing it for action. Your heart (energized by a shot of adrenaline) beats faster. Your breathing quickens and becomes shallower. To give you added nourishment, your liver frees stored nutrients; extra blood carries them to the muscles and brain. This emergency delivery raises your blood pressure. Your eyes dilate, the better to see. Your muscles tighten. You feel tense. You're ready to spring, to act—to fight or flee.

For our ancestors, surrounded by predatory animals and other dangers, this instant mobilization was a biological necessity if our species was to survive. Today, we need to react instantly in sudden emergencies—a car accident, a fire, a burglar in the house. But most of the time the event that stresses us isn't that extreme, and neither is the degree to which our bodies mobilize. Feeling a little stress simply gears us up for the task ahead—studying for an exam, making a sales pitch, dealing with work pressures or whatever.

Just as the brain perceives the need to sound the alarm, so it also recognizes when the stress situation is over and that it's time to demobilize. Jeffrey Rudolph, Psy.D., director of the Multimodal Therapy Institute in New York City, points out that in the normal, healthy rhythm of our daily lives, we go from being fairly relaxed to somewhat stressed (the alarm reaction), then on to a recuperative healing stage (once the stress has passed or we're dealing with it effectively). Eventually we're fairly relaxed, and the cycle can begin again.

When stress becomes *dis*tress, it's because we don't give ourselves that chance to heal or relax—or do so for too brief a time. It happens when we don't cope well with situations that generate stress. It also happens when, being the stressful type, we tend to overreact to situations, or when we feel trapped in high-tension situations. It's this *chronic* stress that's so detrimental to our health.

Setup for Sickness

We've seen how sensitive the body and mind are in reaction to the stresses and strains of life. But it isn't only specific "target organs" like the heart or the respiratory system that are outlets for emotions. Research has shown that much more is at risk when we don't handle stress well—the entire immune system, one of the true keys to physical health, can be seriously affected. When a breakdown of the immune system occurs, it can lead to a range of illnesses that stretches from the common cold to cancer.

The immune system is extremely complex. Simply stated, we're defended against infection and disease by antibodies (protein molecules) that are formed by white blood cells called lymphocytes. Lymphocytes are our stalwart soldiers in the body's fight against the bacteria, viruses, fungi and parasites that are all around us.

Those are the facts doctors have known for years. What's new and different, in terms of the research, is the recognition among clinicians that emotionally disturbing events in our lives can throw the whole immune system out of kilter and leave us vulnerable to a variety of diseases. For example, a clinical team at the Mount Sinai School of Medicine, City University of New York, studied a group of male volunteers, all of whom had wives with breast cancer. What the team did was to test the men's lymphocyte responses before and after their wives died.

What did they find? That there was a "highly significant suppression of lymphocyte stimulation [immune responses]" during these men's first months as widowers. Levels were similar regardless of whether the wife's death was long awaited or occurred with relative speed. Within 4 to 14 months after the death, immune responses went back to normal for some—although not all—of the men.

The fact that men whose wives die lose immunological effectiveness is more than an interesting point of information. Studies show that bereaved spouses—especially widowers—often die an early death themselves. In fact, it's estimated that about 35,000 deaths occur annually among newly widowed people—and that some 7,000 of these deaths may be blamed directly on the spouse's death. Lowered resistance to disease caused by the immensely stressful event of their spouse's death may well be responsible, the researchers believe.

But our resistance to infection and other sicknesses can be weakened by events of lesser magnitude. Something as relatively minor as college stress can do it. In one study, researchers examined dental students' secretion of immunoglobulin A—an antibody that fights off respiratory infections and cavities—periodically throughout the school year. They found a decrease in immunoglobulin A secretion for all students during exams, that high-stress time.

It's clear, then, that when it comes to stress, there is a connection between the mind and the body. In this book, we'll further explore that link. We'll also show you how to determine whether stress is getting the better of you and help you learn how to cope with it.

Test Your Stress Quotient

So you've taken a personal inventory and decided that you're doing just fine in the battle against stress—no ulcers, no migraine headaches, no heart problems or hypertension, just the usual little physical and mental inconveniences that come with life: a rash, muscle aches every now and then, a touch of constipation, more problems with colds and flu than normal, and maybe a bit of forgetfulness and frustration at times. But stress? No problem.

Perhaps you shouldn't be so quick to pat yourself on the back. These minor conditions that are so easily ignored or attributed to other causes may in fact be warning signs that stress is nibbling away at you physically and mentally. If unchecked, a recurring combination of these seemingly innocent conditions could, in the short term, most certainly affect the way you think and feel, and, in the long term, possibly lead to more traumatic problems, such as ulcers, a heart condition or hypertension.

"About eight million Americans have ulcers, or at least that's how many we know about; there are far more people out there suffering from these minor signs of stress who don't realize it," says Edward

1

Charlesworth, Ph.D., a Houston psychologist and coauthor of *Stress Management: A Comprehensive Guide to Wellness.*

Warning Signs of Stress

There are two theories about why most of these minor signs of stress go unnoticed. First, most people have no idea that these common, everyday maladies and behavioral quirks could be stress related, and second, we have become a nation that seems to take pride in denying that something is wrong.

"When you ask people about physical problems associated with stress, most automatically mention headaches," says Mark McKinney, Ph.D., a psychologist in the department of preventive and stress medicine at the University of Nebraska in Omaha. "People don't relate stress to minor symptoms, such as waking at 3:00 A.M. every day and having trouble falling asleep again, or having too many colds. Or they may be working just as hard, and organizing their day, but not getting as much done. They don't associate that with stress either."

Paul Rosch, M.D., president of the American Institute of Stress in Yonkers, New York, says he sees too many people who believe physical and mental problems are "the norm."

"People often think they're supposed to have headaches, back problems, muscular aches and depression," Dr. Rosch says. "They accept these conditions as part of life in the twentieth century."

A stress specialist who spends his days helping people cope with the pressures of living and working in New York City had a firsthand lesson early in his career about the effects of stress. After leaving a small town for life in the big city, Howard Shapiro, M.D., fell in love with a house that he just had to have, even though it was a bit too expensive. Shortly after he decided to buy his dream home, his stomach began to feel queasy, his appetite decreased and his thoughts were foggy at times. One day he went to a movie with friends and lost himself for a few hours in cinematic make-believe, during which time his strange feelings vanished. Shortly after he left the theater, the discomfort returned.

"While I was watching the movie, I was able to relax and concentrate on something that was totally make-believe," he says. "When it was over and my thoughts returned to the real world, my subconscious started letting me know that deep down inside I wasn't too comfortable with the obligation and financial commitment I was about to make.

"I use this example with many of my stress-management patients because when people don't feel well they look for major physical problems. The cause of their discomfort may be subtle and not obvious on the surface, however, and once they realize this, their physical conditions improve." He eventually decided not to buy the house.

Sound familiar? Probably. Consider the following groups of fairly common conditions that you may know all too well.

Lower gastrointestinal distress.   Diarrhea, constipation and flatulence are usually attributed to "something I ate" and rarely to stress, but any one of these three conditions, in combination with other symptoms, often indicates stress, says Dr. Charlesworth. When a 42-year-old woman came to his office complaining of diarrhea, depression, anxiety, sweating and palpitations, tests showed that some of the woman's symptoms were caused by stress, but they also revealed a floppy heart valve. "In this case we were looking for sources of stress and were able to catch the physical problem as well," Dr. Charlesworth comments.

"A bug going around."   As a college undergraduate, Dr. Charlesworth was constantly faced with yet another paper due in a week or a test next Friday. His health always managed to hold up during the days before the assignments were due, but as soon as the paper or test was completed and he was primed for a break, a cold or flu always got in the way.

"The strain had depleted my resistance abilities. My system managed to hold out just long enough so I could do the work, then I'd get sick when it was over because my immunity was low. I used to load up on vitamins, but that made no difference," he says.

Colds, flu and allergic reactions are common, but if you have more than before, the reason could be stress. "If you tax the immune system long enough it will eventually fail, and chances are that you won't have the ability to handle the big problems when they come along," says Dr. McKinney.

Forgetfulness.   No one remembers everything, but forgetting a phone number that you use fairly often, daydreaming excessively or having lapses in concentration may be minor symptoms of stress. A young Louisiana woman who learned relaxation techniques to help cope with other problems in her life found that her concentration improved to the point that she was able to read a book, a task that previously had been impossible.

"Anxiety and stress interfere with the ability to learn and recall, and people who take relaxation training say it sharpens their memory," says Ronald Nathan, Ph.D., of the departments of psychiatry and family medicine at Louisiana State University Medical School, Shreveport, and coauthor of *Stress Management: A Comprehensive Guide to Wellness.*

The most common examples of forgetting under stress come when a student holds test in hand and can't remember a bit of the information that he has been studying for the past five days, or when, upon reaching the podium, a speaker finds that his mind is suddenly blank.

Sleeplessness.   She was an English teacher, a perfectionist who was highly rated by her students and the head of the department. During the summer months she slept like a baby, but when the school bells rang her slumbers were less than golden. She slept fine all through the night on Friday and Saturday, but she barely closed her eyes after the sun set on Sunday, and it wasn't much better Monday through Thursday.

"The stress of getting up and facing another day at school was manifesting itself in her sleep patterns," says Dr. Charlesworth. "She was fine on the weekends."

A bed is supposed to be for relaxation, but experts report that it can be a distressing place for many people. Common problems include difficulty falling or staying asleep, waking at 3:00 A.M. and being unable to fall back to sleep, or insomnia and decreased sex drive, all of which can be induced by stress.

Skin problems and hair loss.   An astute teenager with a keen sense of deduction will tell you that more acne pimples pop out the day before a big date than the day after eating chocolate. Some people are genetically predisposed to skin problems, but acne, rashes and hives are often triggered or aggravated by stress, says Dr. Charlesworth.

Dermatologists have also linked eczema and dermatitis to stress, and a correlation has been drawn to hair loss, as several Houston teenagers found out when the strain of wanting to get ahead and be the best took its toll on their scalps. There were probably telltale signs in the early stages that could have warned of too much stress, says Dr. Charlesworth, who has been involved with several of these unrelated cases, but the stress on these achievement-oriented teenagers went unchecked until bald patches were noticed.

The "Weak-Link" Theory of Stress

One of the most baffling pieces in the stress puzzle is why some people experience a neck ache or decreased sex drive, while others may stutter slightly or have trouble concentrating. The most popular theory points to genetics.

"The body breaks down where it's the weakest, so a weak link in the family history may help determine where stress will show itself," says Dr. Nathan. "If the parents had hypertension or back problems or were prone to muscle-tension headaches, the chances are the offspring will have similar problems."

As a child, a person might have suffered a physical or emotional trauma that could have weakened the body, which could predispose that person to stress-related disorders in that weakened area, he says.

Almost half the population of the United States is ripe for back and muscle problems, says Lyle Miller, Ph.D., a clinical psychologist specializing in stress research at Boston University Medical Center. "About 40 percent of the population has one leg slightly shorter than the other, so these people are automatically susceptible to back problems if stressed."

A weak link could be used as a stress barometer, says Dr. Nathan. For example, a person prone to minor backaches could take preventive measures at the first sign of lower back discomfort and thus possibly avert more serious problems.

Take Stock of Your Stress Symptoms

The best way to recognize that stress is influencing your life is through personal awareness, the experts agree.

"It's similar to knowing when something's wrong with your car," says Dr. Charlesworth. "If you drive it every day, you know when it doesn't sound right or if there's a strange ping. If we study our bodies, we'll be able to tell when something's wrong. We're constantly driving ourselves too hard and not noticing the little things our bodies are telling us.

"It's as simple as watching an exciting movie and noting how your body responds to excitement and tension. Then the next time your body is tense or excited, you'll be familiar with the feelings."

A change in attitude is also in order, Dr. Nathan says. "People don't view stress as a problem. If there's no physical sign, like stomach pain or an ulcer, they don't realize these little symptoms are telling them that corrective action is needed."

Above all, get to the root of the problem, Dr. McKinney emphasizes. Don't just cure the rash or constipation without also considering the stress that could have originally triggered the bodily reactions.

"All you have to invest is a little time. I've never seen anyone waste time learning how to detect and handle stress," he says. "It's like buying an appliance. How much you know can only help you."

Dr. McKinney labels it a consumer issue. "In this case especially, people need to be more responsible for their own health and not leave it in the hands of their physician. The medical community has its hands full curing problems that already exist and doesn't spend much time focusing on prevention."

It also helps to keep an eye on those around you, says Dr. Miller. "When you notice a friend or relative displaying some of these minor signs, tell them. They'll probably bite your head off and tell you to mind your own business, but you'll be doing them a favor in the long run. Wouldn't you want someone to tell *you?*"

If you have only two or three minor stress symptoms, chances are that you're in good shape. Even if you have a combination of symptoms, the experts caution that you shouldn't automatically conclude that an ulcer or heart attack is right around the corner.

There's also the possibility that the symptoms may not be stress related at all. "Diet, hormonal imbalances and other physiological problems can wear the mask of stress or anxiety symptoms," Dr. Charlesworth cautions.

Corrective Action

Once your awareness has been sharpened and you can spot the minor symptoms of stress, the corrective measures are the same as those used for coping with migraines, ulcers, heart attacks and hypertension: relaxation techniques, exercise and other stress-management procedures described in this book.

Time management is another good coping technique, says Dr. Nathan. "People need to establish priorities and set realistic goals. Many of us spend more time planning parties than we do planning our lives.

"But you need to do all of this gradually, and don't get sucked up in the four-day phenomenon, which is very common when people try to make changes in their lives. They're so determined that they diet to starvation and exercise to exhaustion. Then they give up and go back to their old habits."

Adds Dr. Charlesworth, "Ninety-five percent of the U.S. population would benefit from some sort of stress-management training. We need to break the stress spiral by starting with these minor symptoms."

Good Stress: Why You Need It

Your blood pressure climbs, your heart pounds, your body pumps out adrenal hormones. Which are you doing, prowling through a haunted house or laughing at Abbott and Costello?

It could be either. Your body responds to fear and mirth in much the same way—by activating the stress response. That's the curious dichotomy of stress, says William F. Fry, M.D., associate clinical professor of psychiatry at Stanford University School of Medicine.

But while you may be frightened to death, you're unlikely to die laughing. Why? "Because laughter is good stress," says Dr. Fry, a specialist in humor physiology.

In his laboratory studies—where subjects watch old Abbott and Costello films while attached to electronic devices and IVs—Dr. Fry has found that mirth produces an increase in blood pressure, heart rate and a group of substances called catecholamines, the most familiar of which is adrenaline.

On the face of it, mirth seems to trigger the same responses as fear. But there are some differences. The hormones that are secreted are the same, but the actual hormone profile is quite different. With fear, you get a surge of adrenaline. With mirth, says Dr. Fry, "adrenaline responds in a more conservative fashion."

Most important, with laughter, the heart rate and blood pressure eventually drop down to below the original levels, "which is actually very beneficial," says the researcher. Fear, on the other hand, like other forms of distress, can produce lasting damage. (For more on the role of laughter in stress control, see chapter 7.)

It is conceivable that other kinds of "good stress" produce the same beneficial results, suggests Dr. Fry.

"Look at symphony conductors," says Paul Rosch, M.D., president of the American Institute of Stress in Yonkers, New York. "They work long hours, travel frequently, deal with prima donnas and sensitive artists, yet they live long and productive lives. They've got positive vibes going. They enjoy what they're doing, have pride of accomplishment, the approbation of their peers and the applause of the audience — all positive stresses."

And that is the great paradox of stress. How can something bad be good for you? And how can something good be stress? It's all in how you look at it.

Stress or Bliss?

"We think of stress as something that's 'out there,'" says Dr. Rosch. "Well, it's not 'out there.' It's all in how you perceive it. Look at how two people might experience a roller coaster ride. One has his back stiffened, his knuckles are white, his eyes are shut, his jaws are clenched — just waiting for it to be over. The wide-eyed thrill-seeker relishes every plunge and can't wait to do it again."

Researchers Suzanne Kobasa, Ph.D., and Salvatore Maddi, Ph.D., tapped into a figurative roller coaster ride — the breakup of the Bell System in 1983 — to study the personality differences between those executives who stand up to the turmoil of organizational change and those who crumble.

What they found was that the most stress-resistant executives had fewer illnesses — far fewer than might have been predicted by the number of stressful events in their lives — than their more vulnerable counterparts. They also had lower blood pressure and were generally lower in anxiety, depression and suspiciousness, all psychological signs of stress-related strain.

What made these executives stress resistant? Simple. What was stress to others wasn't stress to them. It was opportunity.

"This time in the phone company was highly stressful," says Dr. Kobasa, associate professor of psychology at the graduate school of the City University of New York and coauthor, with Dr. Maddi, of *The Hardy Executive: Health under Stress.* "These people were more likely to perceive the company and themselves in a positive light. In the face of this stress, they saw their work load as highly challenging and more involving, giving them the opportunity to be more independent."

The researchers found that these executives had three characteristics in common—feelings of commitment, control and challenge—which they boiled down to one word: hardiness.

Attitude Makes a Difference

"Hardiness is not the mental counterpart of a strong constitution," cautions Dr. Maddi, professor of behavioral sciences at the University of Chicago. "Rather, hardiness is a set of beliefs people have about the world and themselves and the interaction between the two."

The researchers found that these hardy executives weren't graced with better genes or happier childhoods than the others. They just had better attitudes. High in self-esteem, they thought of themselves and the world as worthwhile. They believed they could influence events around them. And they regarded change, even when it was painful, as an opportunity to learn and grow.

Those three characteristics appear not to eliminate stress so much as defuse it. Without actually changing the objective circumstances, the successful executives were able to transform them into something less stressful simply by changing how they viewed the experience. They truly enjoyed what was clearly overwhelming to others.

Dr. Maddi and Dr. Kobasa have undertaken a study, funded by the National Institute of Mental Health, to examine the effects of "hardiness intervention," a counseling program they developed to teach hardiness, which they believe can be learned at any time in life.

Preliminary results are promising.

"In one study completed with male and female executives, hardiness increased," says Dr. Maddi. "There was a measurable decrease in mental and physical strain, anxiety, depression, suspicion and blood pressure. We also found that there was an increase in immunoglobulin A, a marker of immune response in the upper respiratory area, suggesting a strengthening of the immune system."

Strengthen Your Stress Resistance

The 15-hour hardiness-intervention program relies on three psychological techniques that are fairly easy to master.

Analyze what's *really* bothering you. Participants learn to focus on what is stressful about a particular circumstance— and what isn't—and key in on feelings that may be buried. For example, an anxious executive who can't seem to finish a report in spite of the ominously looming deadline may complain that he "never has enough time to do anything." But, searching his feelings, he may realize that what he feels is fear. Looking at past experiences—grammar-school reports, for instance—he may find that fear of failing is his typical reaction to deadline performance. That new understanding gives him a new sense of control.

Put stress in proper perspective. A technique called situational reconstruction is a form of Monday-morning quarterbacking.

"You ask yourself, how could it have been worse? How could it have been better?" explains Dr. Kobasa. "This is a very powerful device. What you begin to understand is that you do have some skills. When you realize how much worse it could have been, you know you didn't mess up as much as you might have."

Focus on what's going *right*. "Compensatory self-improvement" is designed particularly for those stressful situations that are unchangeable. The theory is that if you can't transform a situation, you can do other things that will give you a sense of commitment, challenge and control. "If your problem is a child with anorexia, you can do very little," says Dr. Kobasa. "But you can make sure that you're doing well at work."

The counseling sessions include a plan of action that is designed by the participant to transform the stress, which, says Dr. Maddi, is far more effective than avoiding it.

Defusing Stress in the Workplace

Because the workplace is so often the source of tension, eliminating unnecessary strain among co-workers is a major part of a productive, stress-free job. Take the close working relationship, for example. When the chemistry's right, few relationships are more satisfying. If you're involved in one, you know that the two of you work better together than either one does separately, as you bounce ideas around, brainstorm and inspire each other.

But what happens when the relationship starts to change or deteriorate? It can be pretty stressful—not to mention what it does to your individual and joint work efforts.

Talking with your associate about why the chemistry's fizzling can be a real chore—you're both busy, so the subject's easy to avoid, and besides, you don't know what you'd say anyway.

Is there any way to figure out what to say beforehand? Experts often suggest writing it down, but there's a crucial element missing in such an exercise: You have no idea what your associate's going to say back.

So we're going to suggest a more novel approach. Try writing a dialogue between the two of you—with you writing both parts. This can be your big moment to indulge your Eugene O'Neill (or Neil Simon, as the case may be) fantasy.

What Dialogues Can Reveal

It sounds crazy, but dialogues can be a terrific tool for figuring out what's going on in a relationship. Besides, they give you an opportunity to rehearse before a serious discussion. When it's only a rehearsal, you tend to be more open and honest. And in trying to anticipate what your colleague might reply to your comments, you might gain some real insight as to how you view that person—or what your part in the problem might be.

A great way to start a dialogue is just to say whatever comes into your head, without consciously or deliberately trying to guide it. The same goes for the words you put into the mouth of your colleague. Here are two examples:

Me: What's wrong with you? I used to be able to count on you for great ideas. Now in meetings, you stare off into space.
Him: I'm bored.
Me: What is so boring? There are a million challenges a day you could run with.
Him: You think so?
Me: Why are you so hostile?
Him: Did you ever stop to think that I'm returning what I get?
Me: You think I'm hostile?
Him: Just listen to yourself. Don't be so defensive.
Me: Is it me? Am I your problem?
Him: You're too busy to be a motivator anymore. You just tell me what I do wrong.
Me: So it is me? Why don't you be a little more honest?
Him: Because you really don't want to hear it. You just want me to stop being bored.
Me: I want you to stop being bored because I'm worried about you.

Although the *Me* character opened the dialogue with a lot of hostility, the subsequent discussion caused him to change his tone completely by the end. Maybe now, when he actually has that big talk with his bored colleague, he'll drop the hostility.

Me: Why is it that every time you come in my office you're hyper?
Him: Hyper? You're the one who's always telling me to be enthusiastic.
Me: But you overdo it. You aren't just enthusiastic. You panic over every little thing.
Him: Panic? That's a new word in your vocabulary. You used to say when I got excited I'd go into overdrive—and that made me work harder.
Me: I don't know, it just drives me crazy now.
Him: I haven't changed. It's you. I'm still the same keyed-up person I've always been. You've just slowed down.
Me: Maybe I have.

The *Me* character starts out complaining, but ends up admitting that what's wrong might be his fault after all.

Balancing Career and Home Life

Now you know one novel way to cope with on-the-job stress. But what about afterward, when you've walked home from the train, tossed your jacket on the couch, sorted through the bills and started to reacquaint yourself with the nonwork people in your life?

No matter how you feel about your job, the transition from office to home is perhaps the most difficult adjustment you make each weekday. While you recover from one set of demands, you immediately confront another. Is there any way to smooth the ride?

Seattle-based psychotherapist and corporate counselor Barbara Mackoff, Ed.D., author of *Leaving the Office Behind,* believes that all of us should first evaluate certain assumptions about our jobs and what they mean.

"We must examine the decision to make work the center of our lives," Dr. Mackoff said. "Careers have to be balanced with personal lives. Many large companies recognize this need—Citibank and American Express are just two corporations that offer work-home and work-parenting seminars.

"As a psychotherapist consultant to major financial and service corporations on the West Coast, I have a front-row seat to observe stresses that people bring home from the office. But I have also had the opportunity to teach business people skills for leaving the office behind." When brought home, office stresses threaten relationships with family and friends, says Dr. Mackoff.

Three Traps to Avoid

The first step in making the transition from office to home easier is to discard three common misconceptions that Dr. Mackoff says lie at the core of much domestic tension.

"My family and friends will understand."   Not as a regular practice, they won't. Sympathy has its limits. No job gives you permission to focus exclusively on yourself. Substitute instead the conviction that time spent with family and friends is sacred and should not be colored by office pressures.

"At home, I can really be myself."   Too often "being yourself" involves rudeness and indifference. The people you live with deserve at least as much consideration as your co-workers. Dr. Mackoff recommends this alternate creed: "At home, I have an opportunity to show the vulnerable, responsive side of myself."

"This is only temporary."   That is, until the next crisis comes along. You can find yourself going from one crisis into another, each time promising your family, "After this, I'll take that vacation, stop working so many hours, etc." But pressure is a way of life in most careers. Don't make it an excuse to take your job out on your family.

How to Leave on-the-Job Stress at the Office

Once you've recognized and discarded these myths, the next step is to develop strategies for leaving stress at the office. Here are Dr. Mackoff's suggestions.

End the day as smoothly as possible.   Slow down. Try tackling your toughest assignments in the morning, when you are fresh. Save easier projects for the afternoon. Deliberately unwind on your way home: Take deep breaths; walk—don't run—to the car; tune in some relaxing music. (Bus and train commuters might want to invest in a portable radio-cassette player, headphones and several soothing tapes.)

Leave unfinished business at your desk.   If you feel you'll spend the evening fretting about it, try this: Toward the conclusion of a busy day, make a list of outstanding tasks. For added relief, imagine the results when every item on the list is completed satisfactorily. Then forget about it until morning.

Maintain perspective.   Despite the day's disasters—you arrived late, spilled coffee on your suit, botched an important presentation and spent an hour trapped in the elevator with your most despised colleague—the world is unlikely to come to an end. If you are still in doubt about this, listen to a news report or scan newspaper headlines. Will today's personal catastrophe matter to you or anyone else in ten years? Probably not.

Cultivate your sense of humor.   "I think people really miss the chance to be silly," remarks Dr. Mackoff. "It's not part of a professional profile." Therefore, using favorite comics as models, write your own inner monologue based on recent office mishaps, sort of a twist on the imaginary dialogue technique mentioned earlier. Think of how much strain you could relieve by viewing your job through the eyes of Joan Rivers or Rodney Dangerfield. (For more on humor, see chapter 7.)

Put a buffer zone between work and home.   Now that you've left work in one piece, you have to come home. Greet your family warmly, but don't hesitate to ask for a few moments alone in order to get reoriented. In *The Executive Parent,* psychiatrist Stephen P. Hersh, M.D., calls this buffer time a physical and emotional necessity that shouldn't be ignored. (Think of how your eyes have to adjust to changes in lighting; similar principles apply here.)

The trick is to allot some time to yourself without making your spouse or children feel rejected. One excellent approach: a quick shower or at least a change of clothes. "Most of the people I talk to are not workaholics; they just have difficulty recovering from the pressures of work," Dr. Mackoff explains. When you trade suit and oxfords for blue jeans and sneakers, you automatically deemphasize work and leave it where it belongs—at the office.

Don't make dinner into an ordeal.

Unless you or your partner finds cooking therapeutic, keep food preparation to a minimum. Let dining itself become a pleasant ritual. Turn off the television and turn on the telephone answering machine. Banish what Dr. Mackoff calls "unwanted guests," like difficult co-workers, from your thoughts and your table. Any references to the day's events should be short and sweet. Better yet, steer conversation toward good books and vacation plans.

Check those managerial impulses.

Rather than switch gears, energetic executives often overschedule their leisure hours. Such behavior is tantamount to setting up shop in the living room. Instead, investigate activities that provide rewards not available on the job: exercise, community service, creative expression, spirituality. Look for something the whole family can enjoy together.

Remove your professional hat as you cross the threshold.

This is a two-way process. You not only have to make an effort yourself; you must also politely discourage friends and colleagues from calling with business questions after business hours. Suggest they solicit advice at a more appropriate moment.

Of course, overhauling your ingrained lifestyle patterns is no simple matter. Expect to lapse into your old habits now and then, especially if you work in an environment where your colleagues take pride in long hours and weekend caseloads, says Dr. Mackoff. This occasional backsliding is the equivalent of snacking on junk food or puffing a forbidden cigarette. Don't give up on yourself entirely because you've veered off course. Allow gradual improvements in your personal life to reinforce your new behavioral program.

When should you seek additional assistance? Dr. Mackoff recommends that anyone who experiences constant "frustration at not being able to effect a smoother transition between work and home" should consider professional help. "If this struggle continues indefinitely, or results in pain, sessions with a qualified therapist can relieve some of the anxiety."

Ironically enough, those who sense no conflict between work and home may be most in need of counseling. "It seems that all of us know someone who works too hard and is too busy working to think about the consequences," Dr. Mackoff observes. "Many of those overachievers have received my book as a gift from people who want to share more of their life after work."

How to Handle a "Problem" Boss

Want to be thin, happy and disease resistant, have low blood cholesterol and a high energy level? Work for a good boss.

That's the voice of science based on several major studies of people's reaction to work stress. In one study of 170 AT&T executives during the tumultuous breakup period, those who felt their bosses were supportive suffered only half as many illnesses as others who believed they didn't have their bosses' backing. The unsupported group was also afflicted with twice the obesity, sexual problems and depression, in addition to their other health breakdowns. And psychological support from bosses was more important to workers' overall health than support from home, the study found.

Even blood cholesterol levels—risk factors for heart disease—climb when employees are under the thumb of an authoritarian fuss-budget, a survey of 357 defense department employees discovered.

A good boss doesn't have to be warm, say the scientists. But he or she must make employees feel they are trusted to work out their own problems.

So what do you do about a "problem" boss? He or she comes into the office at 7:00 A.M. and stays until 7:00 P.M. and expects you to do the same, or undercuts your best efforts, or yells, or takes credit for your work, or sleeps in the kneehole of his desk.

A Five-Point Strategy

Movies like *9 to 5* poke fun at the situation, but in real life a bad boss can create a real health hazard. Here's how the experts suggest you cope.

- Begin looking for another job immediately. That's the word from management consultant Jack Falvey. "Saying 'Everything's great except for this one person' is like saying 'I love living in this house except that it's on fire,' " he warns.
- Until you find a new job, keep out of harm's way. Don't argue or challenge unless you must. Power lies with the boss. You can't win.
- Don't be tempted to try to outmaneuver the boss. Aiming to get the boss fired is more likely to get you fired.
- Keep the relationship businesslike. Avoid the time-consuming and emotionally exhausting games of trying to play up to a bad boss.
- Make the best of it. Praise yourself lavishly for learning lessons in patience, how to handle adversity and what *not* to do when *you're* the boss.

A Remedy for Commuteritis

Do you ever find yourself in the office feeling like you've been through the mill and it's only 9:00 A.M.? Do your eyes hurt, do you feel sleepy or irritable—and you don't know why?

Did it ever occur to you that you may be suffering from commuteritis? Yes, the all-American daily commute. In 1979, the Bureau of Census surveyed heads of households and found they commuted an average of 11.1 miles each way. Millions of us choose to commute so that we can live in the country or take a terrific job offer. And since it's something we do every day, we don't give it much thought. But how many times have you been through this scene?

You're cruising along, catching all the green lights, when suddenly some joker in front of you slows down to ten miles per hour below the speed limit. You change lanes and start to pass, and he speeds up again. You swing back into the right lane behind him. He slows down again. You change lanes again and pull up behind ten cars turning left. He sails through the intersection. You get stuck at the red light.

You fume. You call him names. You swear. You pound your steering wheel.

Not a great way to start the day.

But the stress of a commute isn't limited to bursts of aggravation. It can be a constant, wearing tension that lasts the entire trip and affects your whole body—and you may not even be aware of it. Not aware that when you get tense, you lean forward, straining your back, shoulders, arms and neck. Your teeth clench. Your fingers grip the steering wheel. Your breath comes faster—some people even hold their breath. Your stomach churns.

Creature Comfort behind the Wheel

Highway stress isn't the only factor to consider if you're a daily commuter. Eyestrain or a medication that makes you groggy could be contributing to that feeling of general malaise. You could just be sitting incorrectly behind the wheel. Your body could be so cramped from sitting in one position that it never really wakes up and gets going. So here's a list of hints to help you face the day happier and calmer—even if your morning starts bumper to bumper.

Get your eyes checked.   "If you are feeling tired, headachy, light sensitive—it could be a sign of vision stress," says Melvin Schrier, O.D. The New York optometrist says a daily long drive shouldn't put any undue stress on vision, "as long as the eyes are properly corrected."

Review any drugs or medications that you're taking.   Check with your doctor to be certain that they don't induce sleep or drowsiness. Ask about the interactions between medications and about the effect alcohol might have on them.

The U.S. Food and Drug Administration (FDA) requires drug manufacturers to list possible side effects on over-the-counter drug labels. But this requirement covers only side effects that occur frequently, according to the FDA's Division of Drug Labeling and Compliance. Although a drug may not cause drowsiness in most people, it may affect you. With prescription drugs, the drug makers are required only to include package warning inserts to doctors and pharmacists. It's up to them to pass the word on to consumers. So it's a good idea to ask, in case your doctor or a pharmacist overlooked it.

Adjust your seat properly.   Experts say you should sit high enough to see the ground ten feet in front of the car. Your legs and feet should not be fully extended while driving. Your lower leg should rest at a 45-degree angle to the vertical when the thigh is horizontal. Even if you've pushed the pedal all the way to the floor, your leg should still be slightly bent.

Use your seat belt and harness.   Besides the impressive safety statistics (the National Safety Council says that if all passenger-car occupants used seat belts, at least 12,000 lives would be saved each year), the shoulder harness helps relieve fatigue by holding you in a comfortable, upright position.

Staying Calm en Route

Okay. You're wide awake, comfortable and calm. But you're still in your garage. Now the fun starts. It's fellow commuters that usually cause the big stresses of daily driving.

We asked Lynn Brallier, a psychotherapist, biofeedback therapist and director of the Stress Management Center, Washington, D.C., how she helps clients deal with commuter-related stresses. Brallier is the author of a book about stress, *Successfully Managing Stress.*

"Train yourself to let frustrating situations become triggers to relax. For example, red lights. Some days you seem to catch every one. That's frustrating. But instead of pounding the dashboard and screaming, take a deep breath. Let your shoulders drop. Get out of the anger position. By the time you're finished, the light will be green. Do the same thing with obnoxious drivers."

What about fear of accidents? This is a very real stress for Brallier: She's recovering from a serious traffic accident. "Try a tiny meditation when you get in the car each morning. Program yourself to be alert, to feel safe and protected. And don't drive in front of trucks or cars with dents!"

Brallier also thinks drivers should ask themselves where all that tension is coming from. "It could be deep rooted. Oldest and only children go particularly insane when someone blocks their way or cuts in front of them. They're used to leading the pack, getting their way, being in charge. The youngest child in a family can have the same problem, if he or she has been the center of attention.

"Traditionally, men are more likely to get totally infuriated by traffic than women. Women are more used to being blocked. They're trained to be passive. Of course, these are all old generalizations. Men and women today should both recognize their aggressive tendencies.

"The perfectionist personality or the idealist can also have problems," says Brallier. "You can't have unreal expectations. A lot of people say 'I'm a safe driver. Why can't everyone else drive like I do?' It's never going to happen. Be a little more cynical."

If you haven't recognized yourself in those psychological profiles, there's one more category with which we're probably all familiar: the power-tripper. Domination of the road goads us all on to silly stunts now and then, whether it's racing some guy out of an intersection or forcing a tail-gater to slow down and bug off. "Be aware of your own need for power," says Brallier. "Tell yourself, 'I'm a powerful person—but I don't have to express it at this moment.' "

To defuse highway tension, Brallier thinks diversions like radios or tape decks are great if they help. "Some people say classical music is calming, but listen to whatever you like."

How about working in the car?

"It's fine, as long as it's on a fantasy level—just thinking, brainstorming. It can be a good use of time, if you remain alert to your driving. But leave worrying at work. Stay there to do that type of task."

One final thought on stress and traffic: Heavy loads of stress in your life can actually cause you to be more accident-prone. Stress can make it hard to relax or concentrate on your driving. You may be preoccupied or fatigued. Review the stresses in your life at the moment—life and death changes, job changes, illnesses, money problems. Be aware of those times when you're under heavy stress. Be extra careful on the road. Eat a healthful diet, exercise, stay away from drugs and get enough sleep.

If a large part of your drive is on an expressway or other superhighway, watch out for highway hypnosis. Dr. Schrier recommends that drivers use their eyes and move them around a lot. "Look to the right and left. Check your mirrors. Don't stare. And do it every few minutes."

Unstress Your Love Life

Rita and Lowell are both teachers. They spend their weekdays instructing destructive 11-year-olds, pulling troublemakers out of lunch lines, pulling their own hair out. They shop or run errands on the way home. They exercise, cook dinner, do laundry—and then pass out with a book or the television. Make love on a weeknight? Dream on. Rita and Lowell are too stressed and tense even to think about it.

Marital therapists claim they aren't alone. A great many couples of all ages are finding themselves too stressed to make love at the end of the day. They love each other and they have no major hang-ups. They are simply frazzled and preoccupied with nonsexual problems.

It's true that a loss of interest in lovemaking can be the symptom of a deeper, more complex problem. A man may experience intermittent impotence or a woman might have trouble becoming aroused. These anxiety-producing difficulties might need the help of a professional. But in most cases, relaxation and communication are all that's needed.

Good Friends, but Lousy Lovers

Some say that stress-related celibacy is a sign of our times. Sex therapists report that young, hard-driving, two-career couples who work ten hours a day—the so-called yuppies—frequently lose their appetite for sex. One therapist told us that two of her yuppie clients felt "sexless"—more like roommates than lovers.

But simple biology may explain this trend best. Studies show that people under severe stress, such as soldiers in trenches with shells landing all around, experience a temporary fall in blood levels of sex hormones required for sexual desire. Testosterone decreases in males, while estrogen levels fall in females. Also, some say that we are genetically programmed to respond to stress first and sex later. Given the choice between running from a saber-toothed tiger and dallying with their mate, the caveman and cavewoman would run.

Either way, there are several self-help strategies you might use to help you go from boardroom to bedroom with your sexual desire intact. To be sure, there are no magical cures or foolproof aphrodisiacs—just suggestions from sex therapists about remedies that have worked for people like all of us. For instance:

Don't talk about the day's events; focus on each other.   At least once a week, says Joseph Waxberg, M.D., who is director of the Stamford Center of Human Sexuality in Connecticut, both of you should set a "closing time" at work. Don't hang around the office. Leave for home right away and don't stop anywhere. At home, don't burden each other with bad news. Then put your feet up and relax until dinner. For dinner, do nothing elaborate. Put frozen dinners in the toaster oven and use paper plates and utensils. The important thing is to go slowly and to focus on nothing but each other.

Do something symbolic to help you put a buffer zone between the stressful workday world and your home life.   One physician told us that a friend of his designated a tree by his house to be his "worry tree." Every day after work he "hung" his worries on a branch of the worry tree and left them there till morning. He never brought them inside.

Another man shifts gears between office and home by taking off his business clothes and putting on a pair of comfortable jeans as soon as he gets home. Then he arms himself with a rake or pruning shears and immerses himself in his shrubbery.

Do something wet and wild, like hot-tubbing. Soaking in a hot tub with your mate for a half hour does wonders for relieving stress and fostering intimacy after work, says Iowa City, Iowa, therapist David Rosenthal, Ph.D. When his clients complain of stress, Dr. Rosenthal suggests that they visit Whirling Waters, a spot in Iowa City where a couple can rent a hot tub for $15 per hour, with an option to take a sauna. "People say it's pretty good," he says. "It's a chance to become intimate, with or without sex." If you don't have access to a hot tub, taking a shower together can accomplish the same thing.

Promote sex to a higher place on your list of priorities. Too many people make sex the last thing on their list of things to do during the day—the one that's easiest to sacrifice. Therapist Shirley Zussman, Ed.D., of New York thinks that achieving a good sex life should come before making a lot of money. Too many young couples, she says, "constantly strive for material goodies, like a house in the country. As a result, they constantly feel like they're on a merry-go-round. Their love life as well as feelings of closeness and intimacy suffer."

A good sex life is also fragile, says another therapist, and many people who want to "have it all" forget that sex requires more TLC than other areas of life, like a job or an expensive car.

"Stress can come from two people trying to have perfect careers and private lives. In reality, they're juggling a lot of balls. Unfortunately, the marital/sexual relationship is often the easiest ball to drop," says Barry McCarthy, Ph.D., a marriage counselor at the Washington (D.C.) Psychological Center.

Fine-tune the way you think about sex. West Coast therapist Bernard Apfelbaum, Ph.D., director of the Berkeley Sex Therapy Group in California, has a theory that people who view sex as a goal-oriented performance, during which they must *prove* something, are those whose relations suffer most from outside stresses.

On the other hand, he says, couples who approach sex as a time when they can talk freely with one another about anything they want, and who seek emotional as well as physical intimacy during sex, are those whose sex lives are least vulnerable to the effects of external stress.

If lack of sex becomes a chronic problem, try short-term therapy.   Sex therapists say that almost all stress-related problems can be ironed out with only a few weeks of marital counseling. Therapists typically suggest ways to improve communication at home and to channel stress away from the two of you.

"We explain that many people have this problem," says Don Sloan, M.D., of New York Medical College and Lenox Hill Hospital. "We let them know that they are psychologically normal, that the problem is not the result of a psychosis or neurosis. We use the behavioral approach and emphasize the importance of communication. Usually that is all that is needed."

Take a vacation together.   You've heard the expression, "It's better in the Bahamas"? Now you know what "it" refers to. "A lot of people tell me that sexual activity really picks up on the weekend or on a vacation," says Paul Rosch, M.D., president of the American Institute of Stress. "On a vacation you've got a new and often romantic setting. There's dinner, music, sexier underclothing.

"If you take a look at some resort hotels that cater to honeymooners, you'll find lavish bathtubs, mirrors on the ceiling, fireplaces, round beds and heart-shaped beds. Most of the people who go to these places are *not* honeymooners. Often they are married couples or repeat clients who are trying to recapture that special feeling."

Whatever is bothering you, consider talking about it.   Some people can deal with stress by not talking about it. They just close up until the storm passes. But others need to talk out their stress in order to resolve it. Both techniques are valid.

It's useful, Dr. Zussman points out, for the person under stress to clear the air by saying something like, "Honey, I really feel upset about something. I'm really wound up and I need a chance to cool off." This tactic, if nothing else, reassures the spouse that stress, not lack of love, is the problem.

Another stress-reducing technique, she says, is to switch from the "you" to the "I" mode. Instead of charging that "You did this or that," it's better to say, "I'm upset about this or that." This technique reduces the chance that one spouse will mistakenly think that the other—and not external matters—is the source of the stress.

Be a good listener and don't criticize or give advice. When your spouse decides to ventilate and talk about all of his or her worries, don't interrupt, says Dr. Zussman. The last thing you should do is to give advice on what he or she should have done in that situation. It spoils the ventilation process and blocks the release of stress.

"I had a client who told me that her husband wouldn't talk to her about what was bothering him," she says. "But he said, 'I try to talk, but you don't listen.'" Just listening can do wonders.

Suppose that you *do* put these techniques (or others like them) to work and that you do manage to destress your sex life, what then? For one thing, therapists say, the quality of your marriage is bound to improve. Relaxation and renewed romance won't necessarily save a poor marriage from going on the rocks, but it certainly can't hurt. "There is no marriage that is not made better by a good sex life." says Dr. Sloan. "And there is no marriage that is not made worse by a bad one."

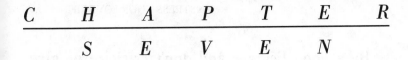

Have a Good Laugh

A few good laughs are a rousing anthem to the soul.

Several doctors and psychologists we spoke to made some encouraging comments about the relationship among a sense of humor, our health and our general enthusiasm for life.

"I find it draining to be around serious-minded people all the time," says David E. Bresler, Ph.D., of the University of California at Los Angeles Medical Center. "Uplifting people uplift others."

We all know people who were brought up without positive reinforcement of their funny bone, as well as others who seem to find humor even in the most serious of situations.

"Eliminate the negative people," suggest other health professionals we spoke with. "Surround yourself with the positive ones—people who fill you with joy and laughter, rather than gloom and doom."

Harry A. Olson, Ph.D., calls that modeling, and it's one of the fastest ways to develop a positive sense of humor. "Humor cannot be taught systematically," says Dr. Olson, a psychologist from Reisterstown,

Maryland, "but must be observed and personally experienced to be mastered."

When was the last time you had a good, hearty belly laugh? You know—the kind where your whole body gets involved. You find yourself thrown against the back of your chair one minute and doubled over the next. Great loud noises burst from your upturned and open mouth. Tears flow from the corners of your eyes, and you grasp the sides of your body in mock agony. At the same time, tense muscles go limp—so much so that at the height of your enjoyment you may not even have the strength to make a fist.

Come to think of it, good, hearty laughter is a lot like exercise—it aids the circulation, massages the abdominal muscles, stimulates digestion, lowers blood pressure and "begets optimism and self-confidence and relegates fear and pessimism to the background." So wrote E. Forrest Boyd, M.D., back in the 1940s. As such, laughter can rejuvenate you much the same as can a few minutes of stretching or a brisk walk.

The Right Kind of Laughter

While there are a lot of situations that may make you laugh, not all of them have uplifting qualities. "Humor as a therapeutic tool must build instead of knock, and therefore excludes sarcasm and cynicism, which pump up the self at the expense of others," says Dr. Olson.

The fact is, *why* you laugh is just as important as *how* you laugh.

"There are three levels of humor," explains Dr. Olson. "Sarcasm is one, but that's destructive. The second, a good pun that gives you a twist of expectancy, has positive qualities. And so does the third level, cosmic humor, which is an appreciation of the paradoxes and absurdities of life.

"The person who has this level of humor is more likely to be flexible and able to take in stride what life dishes out," says Dr. Olson. "I like level three the best for my patients."

So have a good laugh or two today. And while you're at it, make it a point to be good to yourself. That means doing something you especially enjoy and never have time for. Don't keep putting off fun until you have more time, finish this or that project, feel better, or whatever other excuse you can come up with.

Take Comfort in Friends

Confession may be good for the soul, but according to researchers, it may be even better for the body.

James Pennebaker, Ph.D., and Robin O'Heeron of Southern Methodist University in Dallas, Texas, talked to a group of surviving spouses and found that those who confided in others had fewer health problems than those who kept it all in.

"The strain of not confiding emotional burdens of any kind creates great physiological stress," Dr. Pennebaker says. "Not surprisingly, nonconfiders had more stress-related health problems. But they also had more everyday ills, too, like colds and flu.

"Of course," adds Dr. Pennebaker, "whom you confide in is important. If your confidant is in the same social circle, it might make things awkward. A spouse isn't necessarily the right person either, since you may fear hurting his or her feelings.

"Therapists, rabbis or ministers are good to talk to because they are trained to be supportive and nonjudgmental. Sometimes a stranger—someone sitting next to you on a plane—can be a satisfactory confidant."

Of course, the best confidant is a trusted friend.

Friends Act as a Buffer against Stress

Much of what social scientists know about friendships, families and marriages ought to be stamped "Made in Japan."

That's where researchers have found that there is more to a happy, fulfilling relationship than whether it makes you feel all warm and mushy inside. It might also keep you *healthy* inside.

In many ways, the Japanese have much in common with those of us in the West: cigarette smoking, high blood pressure, stress, pollution and crowded cities. Yet the Japanese live longer than any other people on earth, and they enjoy relative immunity from heart disease.

If Japanese and Americans share the same bad habits and environmental stresses, why do the Japanese live longer? Scientists believe the answer lies in Japanese tradition, which fosters close personal ties to friends, family and community.

Studies here in the West lend credence to that theory. Increasingly, new research offers intriguing evidence that those of us who have richer relationships enjoy better health.

"Statistically, this is one of the strongest areas under study," says S. Leonard Syme, Ph.D., professor of epidemiology at the University of California at Berkeley and one of the world's leading experts on relationships. "What isn't clear is how it works. How does a relationship get into the body and influence biological processes? All we know at this point is that something very important is happening."

Dr. Syme, working with Lisa Berkman, Ph.D., coauthored what many consider to be the definitive study on social ties and the risk of death. What Dr. Berkman and Dr. Syme discovered was compelling. They found that socially isolated people—those who were unmarried, divorced or widowed, those with few close friends and few church or social contacts—were almost three times more likely to die of a wide variety of diseases than were people who enjoyed happy, fulfilling social lives. Without a safety net of close personal relationships, they discovered, we become more vulnerable to disease.

Considering how lonely life would be without our friends and loved ones, the fact that they might also save our lives is an incredible bonus. Further studies have lent dramatic support to the theory offered by Dr. Berkman and Dr. Syme.

How to Enrich Your Relationships

The Beatles, it seems, weren't far from wrong when they sang, "Love is all you need." The best medicine we could possibly "take" doesn't come in a bottle and can't be injected through a hollow needle. It flows through our relationships with the most important people in our lives. Finding ways to open up to these special people could be the single most important thing you will ever do.

But it takes work. When it comes to building a deeper, more loving relationship, we need to learn and use some important skills.

Be selective.   This is not to say some people are worthwhile human beings while others are not. But if you want lasting relationships, you'll have to devote the most energy to the ones that matter the most to you.

"I'm a man with a cardiac condition, so I'm very impatient," says Gerald M. Phillips, Ph.D., professor of speech communications at Pennsylvania State University and coauthor, with H. Lloyd Goodall, Jr., of *Loving and Living.* "Time is very important to me. I won't waste time on people who annoy or bother me. You only have so much time on earth, so you might as well spend it on quality relationships."

Open up to others.   "The key to all relationships is honest communication," says Richard Grossman, director of the Health in Medicine Project at Montefiore Medical Center in the Bronx and author of *The Other Medicines.* "So open up communication. Tell people what you really feel. It doesn't have to be a verbal message. It can be written. Send a letter. Call three friends you haven't heard from for a while. Take responsibility for communication. Openness is natural. We have the capability."

Cultivate the art of small talk.   If you're at a cocktail party, and you are approached by a loud, opinionated political "expert," small talk is a handy way to dismiss him without hurting his feelings — if he has any.

As a preliminary to deeper, more meaningful conversation, though, small talk has a larger purpose. It's a reassuring ritual that lets you know that your friend cares about you and vice versa. After "How's the job?" and "How are the kids?" you're free to discuss what's really going on in your life.

Put the interests of the relationship first.   If husband and wife have conflicting needs—he wants a job in New York, she wants to stay on the farm in Oneonta—both of you should consider what's best for both of you, not one of you.

This is one of the "trade secrets" of happily married couples, according to psychologist Florence W. Kaslow, Ph.D., president-elect of the American Psychological Association's Division of Family Psychology and director of the Florida Couples and Family Institute.

"There's a fine balance between 'what's good for me' and 'what's good for the relationship,'" says Dr. Kaslow. Happily married couples manage to achieve that balance. "It's not only happy," adds Dr. Kaslow, "it's healthy. It's problem-solving with a mutual concern."

Work together.   You've probably noticed that some of your best friendships evolved out of a shared task, like building a tree house at the local elementary school or planning a block party. "When I was a child, I lived in an area of the country that was prone to flooding," says Dr. Syme. "And I remember once, when I was about 11, working day and night for three days, filling sandbags for flood control, along with my friends and my neighbors. It was a highlight of my life.

"The best times I've ever had in my life were times I've worked with other people. It didn't matter whether it was a good occasion or a miserable one."

Overlook the warts.   "If the relationship isn't working, people think there must be something wrong with the person they're related to," says Dr. Phillips. "There must be a flaw."

But if the relationship is faltering, it could be because you have unrealistic expectations. You expect your friend, lover or husband to be perfect. If you really want the relationship to grow, you'll cut out the pedestal routine.

"What you get out of a relationship is really so important that you will learn to put up with or ignore little things about your partner that bother you," says Dr. Phillips.

Share everything—even the sad stuff.   It sounds trite, but the relationships between couples and among friends that survive happily from one year to the next are those in which there are no restrictions on feelings.

There's no rule that says we should share only the good feelings and thoughts with our pals and mates. That's just half a loaf, and in this case half a loaf is no better than crumbs. When unhappy events bring you down, it'll make you feel better just to share those feelings with someone who loves you. You aren't burdening anyone. In any case, your husband, wife, son, daughter or best friend all know that when the world gets the better of them, you'll be there to hear their sad stories, too.

"Finding someone to share your weaknesses with is very important," says Dr. Phillips. "If you don't, you'll drown in them."

And that, he adds, is one of the most important things you need to know to take your sleepy relationships and turn them into something almost miraculously life-giving.

"I've had physicians tell me six times in my life, starting at age 11, that I only had a year to live," says Dr. Phillips. "I'm still here. I've proven all the doctors wrong, and I think that's because I have wonderful friends all over the country who help me along when I'm having a hard time. And they know that the love goes both ways. When they need similar treatment, they know they can cash their chips with me."

If you have a problem that's more than you can handle on your own or that you can't share with your closest confidant, consult chapter 15 for crisis counseling services.

Emotional First Aid

At some time in their life, everyone suffers the type of emotional wound that can take months or years to heal. The loss of a friend, the death of a loved one or a divorce all modify life in far-reaching and unalterable ways.

The vast majority of life's emotional hurts, though, are little ones—the garden-variety upsets that can leave you rattled for a day or two. Still, who wants to waste even one day on negative emotions? And the more hassles we have to deal with, it seems, the more disturbed we are likely to be by the *next* little incident that comes along.

How can you stop those emotional cuts and scrapes from turning into a major malady? By stocking your mental medicine chest with a handy supply of Band-Aids for the soul.

An Emergency Kit for Stress

We compiled a list of some typical, everyday upsets, and we asked psychologists for their tips on how to make a quick recovery. Their suggestions are specific, but the underlying principles can be applied to most of the common hassles you might encounter.

Getting caught in traffic.
"There are three general strategies for dealing with that type of situation," says Robert D. Kerns, Jr., Ph.D., assistant clinical professor of psychology in psychiatry at the Yale University School of Medicine. "The first is behavioral—*doing* something to minimize the frustration. If you're caught at a traffic light, for instance, you can turn on the radio to distract yourself, or roll down the window to get a breath of fresh air.

"The second type of strategy is called cognitive, which refers to what you *think*. For example, tell yourself positive statements. If you're late for an appointment and get caught at a traffic light, you can tell yourself, 'I'll make it, it's only one light, it only lasts 60 seconds.' You can even count the seconds.

"Another cognitive strategy is to distract yourself by thinking about a different, more pleasant scene. You can imagine what you'll do to relax at the end of the day, or imagine walking in your yard, looking at the garden."

If you really are going to be late, you might want to take a slightly different approach. "In that case, it's probably not the traffic jam that's causing you distress, but anticipation that something awful or catastrophic will happen later because of being late," says Dr. Kerns, who is also chief of the counseling and health psychology section at the Veterans Administration Medical Center in West Haven, Connecticut. "Rehearsing how you're going to cope with that future situation is a positive way to distract yourself. You might decide to make a joke about catching every red light, make a simple apology or just be ready to get down to business when you do arrive. That's a useful way to spend that time.

"The third strategy is to use relaxation techniques to minimize your emotional distress or the physiological arousal associated with it. Sit comfortably in your seat and relax all of your muscles very quickly until you become like a rag doll, or close your eyes for 15 seconds."

The left-out feeling.
Have your friends ever forgotten to invite you to an outing? Have you ever had a birthday that nobody

remembered? Has your son or daughter ever forgotten to send you a card on Mother's Day?

"It's important to recognize that at one time or another everyone has forgotten a date, forgotten to send a card or to call," says C. Eugene Walker, Ph.D., professor of psychology at the University of Oklahoma College of Medicine in Oklahoma City and author of *Learn to Relax*. "We all fall down. There probably isn't a person who hasn't done it or had it happen to him. You have to realize that it's just a part of life."

"It's not the fact that you didn't get the card that's so upsetting," Dr. Kerns says, "but the negative thinking that goes along with it. A person prone to becoming distressed by those situations will go into a whole internal tirade about the event—all of the awful things that are meant by it. They'll say, 'This means they don't think of me, don't care about me, don't love me.' They'll think back to similar situations in the past that brought about similar feelings and they'll dwell on them. Psychologists refer to that type of thinking as negative cognitive distortion. It's common in people with depression.

"The strategy for dealing with that is to catch yourself early on in the phase of negative thinking and try to stop it," Dr. Kerns says. "Not by saying, 'Don't think that,' because as soon as you say, 'Don't think about X,' you're going to think about X more and more. What you really want to do is think of positive statements—a different way of evaluating the same situation. You can say, 'Maybe the card is late. I've sent late cards before. I can probably expect it later in the week. And if I don't get one, it's not the end of the world.' The idea is to minimize negative thinking by thinking more rational thoughts."

An overloaded schedule.   When your schedule has you swamped and you're ready to set fire to your office, you can use these pointers to get you back on an even keel.

"First, you need to be realistic about what you can get done," says Robert Felner, Ph.D., director of training in clinical psychology at Auburn University. "Don't say, 'I'll work 40 hours straight and finish everything.'

"One of the best ways to approach a work overload is to map out exactly what you've got to get done and prioritize the list. There's no way to deal with a general work overload, but you can deal with each of ten tasks individually. That way, at the end of the day you can look at what you've accomplished instead of feeling like you've failed. There are too many people who spend a day being very productive and go home feeling like they didn't get anything done because everything isn't finished."

"Schedule breaks—periods of reward at each step along the way," suggests Dr. Kerns. "Tell yourself that you will make it through. Appreciate that you've made it through similar situations before and that you'll do it again."

A marital spat. If a fight with your spouse ruffles your feathers for a whole day, you may want to learn some strategies for smoothing things out more quickly.

"I can really be affected by marital spats," says Stephen D. Fabick, Ed.D., a clinical psychologist from Birmingham, Michigan. "One thing that helps me is just realizing that it's going to happen every so often. You can't have your happiness totally dependent on whether you and your spouse are getting along that day. And you can't judge your relationship by it either."

"It's important to make plans for solving the problem," says Dr. Walker. "It's very disturbing to leave a problem open or unsettled. Propose a strategy and make a date to discuss it later." That way, it's easier to get on with your day.

"You might want to plan to do something special when you get home to make up," says Dr. Kerns. "That's a more positive way to think about it."

Performance jitters. Most people are familiar with that fluttery feeling they get in their stomach when they have to give a speech, take a test or go to a party at the boss's house. That feeling is often more distressing than the actual event.

"That's referred to as anticipatory anxiety," explains Dr. Kerns. "It's not so much the doing of the task that's so anxiety producing, but the anticipation of it—the ruminating about it. We tend to think about the event in ways that provoke intense anxiety. The result is butterflies in the stomach, a headache or other symptoms.

"A good strategy is to realize that you are responsible for what you're doing to yourself and that you have the ability to control those feelings," he says. "You can say, 'It's not the situation—it's my thinking about it that's generating the anxiety. I'm responsible, I'm in control and I'm able to do something about it.'

"If it's a speech you're giving, you can organize your talk and practice it. If it's a social engagement you're dreading, you can think about who'll be there and mentally rehearse what you might say to them.

"You can also use relaxation techniques," recommends Dr. Kerns. "They'll reinforce your feeling of control because you'll see that you have the ability to do something. But there's also a physiological rationale for doing them. They literally loosen your muscles, slow your heart rate and control your blood pressure."

The most widely prescribed relaxation technique is progressive muscle relaxation. You do it by systematically tensing and relaxing the various muscle groups in your body to generate a sense of total body relaxation. Deep, regular, diaphragmatic breathing can also help you relax. The shallow chest breathing we do most of the time seems to go along with anxiety.

Another good relaxation technique is called positive imagery. That's where you imagine a relaxing scene, using as many senses as possible. "A beach scene works well for me," Dr. Kerns says. "I imagine being alone on the beach, watching the waves rippling, hearing the sound of the waves breaking on the shore, tasting a hint of salt in the air and feeling the warm sun and sand. Some people like to imagine walking through the woods on a crisp fall day. For others, sitting in a rowboat on a lake with a fishing line is very relaxing. Whatever your scene is, the more elaborate and detailed you make it, the more relaxing it will be." (For more on relaxation techniques, see chapters 10, 11, 12, 13 and 14.)

"You should also recognize that anxiety is part of life," says Dr. Walker. "That's much less upsetting than having the attitude that it's terrible and you shouldn't have to feel it."

In fact, you may even be able to put that anxiety to good use. "Up to a point, anxiety can really help people," says Dr. Fabick. "If we realize that, we can use it to our advantage. Many actors and actresses say that they get nervous, but it helps them get up for the performance. If you accept the normalcy of the anxiety and harness the energy in a positive way, it can help you."

Your big plans fell through. Have you ever looked forward to something, like a vacation or a visit with your family, and had it fall through at the last minute? Maybe you were planning for it, dreaming about it, and when it fell through it left you feeling a little blue.

"It's important to realize how understandable it is that you would feel disappointed," says Dr. Kerns. "You don't want to cover it up with Pollyanna-ish statements. But it's also important to put it in perspective."

"You can do things to be good to yourself to reduce the disappointment," suggests Dr. Felner. "Try doing a couple of little things that are fun. Sometimes people punish themselves after a disappointment and don't do anything. That just makes things worse. You can say, 'Gee, I won't get to go to the Bahamas this year, but I can take a couple of side trips. And there are a lot of fun and productive things that I can do around here.' "

"It's great to get excited," says Dr. Fabick. "But with any expectation you've got to keep in mind that you can't count on things always working out. You don't want to go to the other extreme, though, where you never get excited about anything. The healthiest people seem to be able to find some balance of realistic expectations, keeping in mind that Murphy's Law [If anything can go wrong, it will] is always operating.

"Another preventive measure is having several options. Many times we become so focused on just one possibility that if it falls through we become despondent."

A long-distance family fight. With family members already living in distant places, a fight can make you feel light-years apart. And feeling cut off from your loved ones can be terribly distressing.

"The first thing to do is take a breather," says Dr. Kerns. "Take a brief period of time to cool off. But the bottom line is to reestablish contact soon. The worst thing is to avoid further contact with the person. That only potentiates the feelings of guilt, sadness, anger and distrust. Reviewing the fight in your mind will also amplify the distress you're feeling and make you more likely to avoid a person that you care about. When you keep in contact, though, there's always the possibility of working things out."

"Be active at problem-solving rather than letting things sit and fester," agrees Dr. Felner.

"Think through what has happened, how you would want it to

come out, and what you can do to remedy the situation," he suggests. "You can seek support from friends to calm yourself and get ideas."

You've lost your temper.   Have you ever gotten so angry that you've felt dangerous? Or has one of your outbursts left you feeling shaken, scared or even guilty?

First off, step back. "Instead of trying to justify your anger, take steps to reduce it," suggests Dr. Felner. "Don't act on that anger. Instead, sit down, take deep breaths and try to relax. Most people find that when they're involved in an argument, if they can get out of the same room for 15 minutes, they're okay. They just need that time to pull back and calm themselves."

"It's a good idea to discharge the energy physically by taking a brisk walk or by participating in some other form of exercise," says Dr. Fabick. "And realize that it's normal sometimes to want to choke somebody. Don't feel guilty about it—just don't do it."

Parent-teenager conflicts.   Anyone who's lived with a teenager probably knows what life on a roller coaster is like. One minute everything's fine and the next minute your child is screaming, "I hate you!" Maybe you even scream back.

"At times like those, your strongest link is with the other parent," says Dr. Kerns. "It's important to reach out to that person for support and to align with them.

"The pain you can feel in that situation is not simple to deal with. You might be able to minimize it, though. If you know full well it's a temporary thing, tell yourself that. Don't overdramatize it—keep it in perspective. You can say, 'He's not lost forever; we'll get over it in the next few days.' You can see it as just one upset in a long line of events and seeming catastrophes in raising a child. It starts in infancy and continues all the way through."

"If *you've* gone overboard, acknowledge your own regret. And address it if the teen has, too," says Dr. Fabick. "Kids do well with parents who have the strength to admit mistakes."

Dr. Felner agrees. "It's unfortunate that parents have been fed all that stuff about consistency being more important than everything else. If you've lost your temper, you can apologize. Sometimes in a rage a parent might tell a kid that he's grounded for a month. If it's unreasonable, you can go back and say, 'Look, I was angry and upset. I

said the wrong thing. You're only grounded for two days. I'm sorry.'
You'll both feel better."

   A brief note of caution: These suggestions are meant to help you
keep your composure when faced with normal, everyday hassles. If any
of these situations pose serious problems for you, you may also want to
seek professional help.

Stretches to Short-Circuit Stress

Dealing with the long-term effects of stress requires long-term strategies. But what can you do about the short-term stuff—like when your boss insists that you've got to have a big report done by yesterday, or when you've just fixed the toaster and the washing machine blows up?

Stretch, that's what. In addition to mental and emotional reactions, stress produces physical reactions. Chances are, if you're under stress, one or more of your muscle groups is working overtime and needs a break. In fact, the first place stress usually shows itself—even before the headaches begin—is in your muscles.

So the next time you need quick relief from stress at home or at work, pull up a chair and try a few of these simple exercises recommended by Charles T. Kuntzleman, Ed.D., national program director of Fitness Finders, Inc., and author of *Maximum Personal Energy.*

Before you begin, keep in mind that these exercises are a stopgap solution only. The most effective stress reducer is a systematic and regular program of aerobics and stretching. Physically fit people are generally more effective at coping with stress. Also, there's a proper way to do *any* stretching exercise, and Dr. Kuntzleman describes it this way:

1. Using gentle, slow, deliberate movements, go to the point where you feel a tug and hold that position.
2. Visualize the muscle relaxing and stretching at the point of the tug.
3. Stretch again until you feel the tug. Begin by holding for 10 seconds, then gradually increase to a maximum of 30 seconds.
4. Relax and return to your starting position. Each of these exercises should be done from a sitting position and should be repeated two or three times. Breathe as normally as possible, but with your mouth open.

For the Neck

Stress can settle into your neck. To get out the kinks, try these exercises.

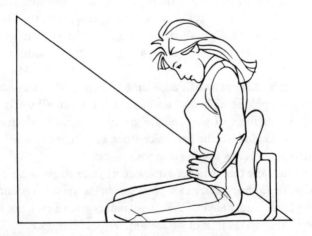

Neck Stretch.   Draw your head down toward your chest as if you were trying to nibble the buttons off your shirt.

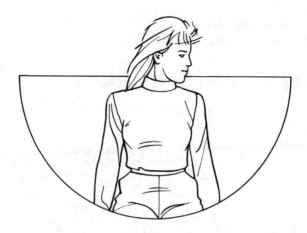

Neck Turn.   Look over your left shoulder, then look over your right shoulder.

For the Shoulders

If you feel the effects of stress in your shoulders, here's one way to relax it away.

Shoulder Shrug.   Draw your shoulders up toward your ears as if you were trying to gesture an enormous "I don't know." Then relax and drop your shoulders down farther than normal. (The upward motion contracts the muscle, but it helps you relax more once you begin the stretching part of the exercise.)

For the Shoulders and Neck

To release tension in your shoulders and neck, try these simple maneuvers:

Elbow Waggle.   Clasp your hands behind your head; draw your elbows forward, then draw your elbows backward.

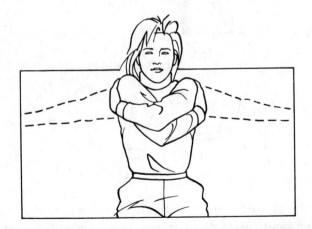

Wraparound.   Extend both arms directly out to the sides from your shoulders, so that they are parallel to the floor and form a straight line from fingertips to fingertips. Keeping your arms parallel to the floor, draw your hands back as if you were trying to touch them behind your back. Then bring your arms back across the front of your body and give yourself a hug.

For the Lower Back

The lower back is a common site for tension buildup. These three stretches can help defuse tension there.

Palms Down.   Sit on the floor with your legs stretched out in front of you. Bend forward at the waist and try to put the palms of your hands flat on the floor. (If you can already do that, try sliding your hands forward along the floor until you reach the point of tug.)

Shin Clasp.   Raise one knee up and clasp the leg by the shin with both hands. Bend forward and try to put your head on your kneecap and your chest on your thigh. Repeat with your other leg.

Shoe Stretch.   For people who have knee problems, this is an alternative to the Shin Clasp. Extend both legs in front of you with both heels flat on the floor. Slide both hands down one leg and try to touch your shoe. Then reach for the opposite shoe with both hands.

For the Legs

Calves and thighs tense up when you sit still for hours. Try this:

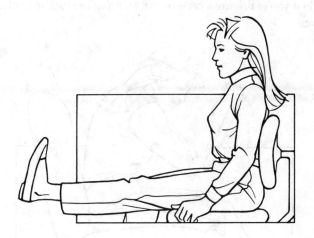

Leg Lift.   While sitting in a chair, make sure your back is against the back of the chair, then raise one leg until it is parallel to the floor. Try to curl your toes back toward your body as much as possible. Then raise your leg upward. Repeat with your other leg. (This exercise has the double benefit of stretching the calves and hamstrings while conditioning the abdominal muscles.)

For the Car

All of these exercises are suited for the home or office, but what do you do if you're driving a car—or worse, if you're stuck in traffic? Try this one:

Modified Angry Cat.   With both hands grasping the top of the steering wheel, place your forearms on the wheel also. Make sure your lower back and buttocks are against the back of the seat. Then bend your upper body forward and arch your back like an angry cat.

Remember, for all stretching exercises: tug, visualize, hold, return.

Exercise, the Supreme Tranquilizer

As you move through your day, there's a good chance you'll have more than one opportunity to get angry: a chance encounter with an infuriating person, a fender bender in heavy traffic, perhaps a slow elevator. If the rage comes and goes, you're probably okay. But if the feelings persist and you don't vent some steam, your body responds by pumping out a potentially toxic substance that's been linked to heart problems and stroke.

The substance is called noradrenaline, and it, along with adrenaline, is triggered into action by the brain when you sense trouble or a threat. These hormones send blood rushing to the muscles, preparing you for swift action (this is commonly known as the fight-or-flight response). A problem arises when you stay angry and don't vent the hostility, because the brain keeps triggering noradrenaline, which, besides threatening the heart, may also hamper the immune system.

"Everyday stressors can cause the release of this hormone," says Redford Williams, M.D., of Duke University Medical Center in Durham, North Carolina, an internist who's studied the hazards of hostility. "In

53

lab experiments, we've found that noradrenaline can be released when people are given a difficult math problem to solve. It's very easily discharged, especially in today's society where there are so many potential irritants."

It's also easy to deal with. "If you blow up and vent your feelings, then you're releasing your anger, and, in most cases, everything inside will go back to normal and the hormonal release will stop," says Dr. Williams. "Any physical expression that uses up calories, such as exercise, burns up the hormones instead of allowing them to get to the stage in the body where they can do harm. In this case, physical exercise is actually relaxing."

How Exercise Burns Off Excess Tension

"Exercise is emotional aerobics," says Bob Conroy, M.D., a psychiatrist at the Menninger Clinic in Topeka, Kansas, where he organized a cardiovascular fitness program that boosts sagging spirits. "You don't have to run marathons, either. Any good aerobic routine that speeds up heart and breathing rates, carried on a minimum of three times a week for 30 minutes each session, pays big dividends."

Indeed, new studies and clinical evidence suggest that such an aerobic program can build emotional hardiness in at least nine ways.

- It energizes.
- It relieves tension and anxiety.
- It strengthens the body's stress-coping mechanism.
- It counteracts hostile, Type A behavior.
- It clears the mind, improving concentration and memory.
- It encourages a more positive self-image and improves self-confidence.
- It contributes to feelings of exhilaration and physical well-being.
- It improves sleep.
- It alleviates depression.

Some of the effects can be explained quite simply. The energizing effect, for example, is the result of improved body efficiency, says Kenneth Cooper, M.D., M.P.H., in his book *The Aerobics Program for*

Total Well-Being. Like a well-tuned engine that uses less oil and gasoline, a well-tuned body uses less energy to perform daily functions.

Stress Resistance and Your Heart

Toned muscles make every movement—from lifting a pencil to walking up a flight of stairs—relatively effortless. And a conditioned heart—which pumps more blood with each stroke—doesn't have to work as hard, circulating the same volume of blood with fewer strokes.

The lower resting heart rate is a key benefit of aerobic conditioning. And the effect is usually noticeable after just a few weeks of regular workouts. In one study of middle-aged men, Dr. Cooper reports, heart rates dropped from an average of 72 beats per minute to 55 beats per minute after a three-month training program. This not only provides the exerciser with increased stamina but, as Dr. Cooper explains, it also offers a form of stress resistance.

"Better cardiovascular fitness tends to put a 'governor' on the effect that the adrenal gland's secretions can have on the heart. In response to intense emotions, anxiety or fear, the resting heart rate increases to some extent. This is the result of the outpouring of adrenaline into the body. The adrenal gland stimulates the heart to beat faster and thus prepares us for 'fight or flight,' " he says.

A fit person subject to stress will still experience a rise in heart rate, but not to nearly the extent that a sedentary person would. Dr. Cooper cites two related studies to demonstrate this point. One study measured the heart rate of a sedentary elementary school teacher at rest (75 beats per minute) and in action, teaching her class (95 beats per minute). Another study made similar measurements on a very fit male college instructor. By comparison, his resting heart rate was 65 beats per minute and his teaching rate rose to just 67 beats per minute. Even in the throes of a heated argument with a student, he was clocked at just 70 beats per minute.

How does this translate into benefits?

"A lower heart rate during stress means you tend to stay calmer and more in control of your emotions. But there are even more important consequences. To put it bluntly, a well-conditioned heart may save a person's life," says Dr. Cooper, citing several cases in which unfit people succumbed to sudden heart attacks following emotionally taxing ordeals. "Chances are, if [they] had been in good aerobic condition, [they] could have tolerated that stress and would still be alive today."

Exercise Reduces Anxiety and Fear

Of course, you don't have to wait for a crisis to feel the effects of your effort. Every time you work out hard, you're helping to release pent-up tension. Immediately afterward, you'll feel relaxed, refreshed and energized. As evidence of this, a study of 15 men demonstrated that a 15-minute aerobic workout was sufficient to reduce anxiety to below preexercise levels. The tests showed the men to be more relaxed, not only immediately following their workout but also 20 minutes later.

To get the most stress-reducing benefits from your fitness program, Dr. Cooper advises that you schedule your workouts after work and before dinner. At that time, exercise helps release tensions that have accumulated during the day. As a bonus, he says, exercising at this time is a sort of appetite depressant—good news for weight watchers.

The calming power of exercise is really put to the test in the treatment of phobias, one of the most anxiety-provoking problems we know of. But, not surprisingly, this unlikely therapy passes with high grades. According to several reports, running reduces the anxiety associated with irrational fears ranging from agoraphobia (fear of open spaces) to claustrophobia (fear of closed spaces). Exercise therapy is particularly effective when combined with visualizations of pleasant fantasies, it is noted. In fact, one study demonstrates that running and fantasizing are as effective as standard desensitization (which attempts to reduce a fear by increasing exposure to the stress trigger).

Building Confidence with Sweat

While exercise is reducing anxiety levels to new lows, it's raising confidence quotients to all-time highs.

"One case that comes to mind involves a woman who was a classic introvert," says Dr. Cooper. "For example, she always stayed in the background in conversations and social gatherings and was so self-conscious that she would never have been seen on a track running in shorts. But then she became involved in our programs at the Aerobics

Center, and immediately her attitude changed. She began to run regularly, performed exceedingly well on the treadmill stress tests and completely reversed her personality traits.

"One of the things that can be most easily documented about people's responses to our exercise programs is an improvement in self-image," he adds. "And along with an improved self-image, I have come to expect a transformation of the person into an outgoing, self-confident personality."

Studies on the attitudes of elderly people likewise show that those who exercise feel better about themselves than those who don't. On a psychological test designed to measure a person's self-image, people who exercised the least felt that they didn't live up to their ideal image of themselves. Those who exercised the most showed a good body image, close to their desired image of themselves.

A chief factor in this, says John H. Greist, M.D., a psychiatrist and professor at the University of Wisconsin, is what he calls capacity for change. "Runners learn, often dramatically, that they can change themselves for the better. Running improves physical health, appearance and body image, and also increases self-acceptance."

In addition, Dr. Greist says, a regular fitness program builds strong character traits in at least three other areas:

Mastery. "Individuals who become independent runners develop a sense of success and mastery of what they perceive as a difficult skill."

Patience. "To become an independent runner takes time, and one learns the necessity of patience and making regular efforts until running becomes a habit."

Positive habit. "Some patients recognize running as a positive activity and consciously substitute it for more negative and neurotic defenses and habits such as smoking, drinking, overeating and nonproductive arguing."

"Depressed people feel better about themselves after becoming runners," says Austin Gontang, director of the San Diego Marathon Clinic. "Initially, a person might feel that 'I can't do anything' or 'I can't go on.' Running takes that negative energy and turns it around—the person *can* go on. Maybe for five more miles!"

Psychiatrist Thaddeus Kostrubala, M.D., author of *The Joy of Running,* agrees. "Running works because it changes the personality patterns," he says. "People develop a greater sense of their own value. They feel better about themselves. They feel an increased sense of personal strength."

"We know now that personality in adults is a dynamic thing, not a static thing," says A. H. Ismail, M.D., professor of physical education at Purdue University, who is a former Olympic basketball player. "There can be changes, and the changes that are produced through a fitness regimen are in a positive direction." For over 20 years, Dr. Ismail has been conducting fitness programs involving hundreds of participants and has found that those who scored low on emotional stability tests before exercising showed marked improvement after completing a fitness program.

"Type A's" Benefit Most

The results of a Duke University study seem to bear this out. According to researcher James Blumenthal, Ph.D., and associates, participation in a regular exercise program can modify one of the toughest—and most self-destructive—personality patterns known: the hard-driving, coronary-conducive Type A behavior.

It's hard to say why exercise has such a marked effect on personality, Dr. Blumenthal admits, but "the decision to exercise could be related to an overall reevaluation of lifestyle behaviors and a change in values. It's difficult to document whether or not the pervasive 'I feel so much better' is a function of exercise, the group setting or time. But people doing something they know is good for them—and they can tell that quickly just by walking up two flights of stairs without being so winded—experience a positive feeling of accomplishment."

Take Two Deep Breaths and Call Me in the Morning

You breathe 11 times per minute, not the usual 16 to 20. Each breath takes in about 5 percent less oxygen, and each exhalation contains less carbon dioxide. Your heart rate slows by about three beats per minute and your blood pressure decreases. Your skin resistance — the same measurement that's taken during a lie detector test — is some 300 times higher than normal, a sign that anxiety is at an absolute minimum. Blood flow to the brain increases by 25 percent. Even the electrical activity of your brain changes. The "brain waves" that usually flow at random become a synchronized and even field. And the alpha waves, which are associated with a feeling of relaxation and well-being, increase in frequency. But you're not trying to do any of it. It's all happening naturally, easily.

You're simply practicing a meditation or relaxation technique that activates your body's own relaxation response.

First described by Herbert Benson, M.D., a cardiologist and associate professor of medicine at Harvard Medical School, the relaxation response is our protective mechanism against overreaction to stress.

Physiologist Mary Asterita, Ph.D., of the Indiana University School of Medicine, explains: "In the stress response, you escalate the sympathetic nervous system. In the relaxation response, you deescalate the sympathetic nervous system. In the stress response, your pupils dilate, your hearing becomes more acute, your blood pressure increases, your heart rate increases, your respiration rate increases, your circulation changes and moves away from the periphery (into the muscles and vital organs), and you become pale. These are just some of the physiological responses that may occur. The relaxation response is the exact opposite."

It's no wonder, then, that people who regularly practice a relaxation technique, like meditation, are less anxious and tense and better able to resist stress. They also report feeling happier — more optimistic, self-confident, energetic and productive. Research has demonstrated that the relaxation response can counter the cumulative impact of stress on your health.

A few years ago, for example, over 150 employees of the New York Telephone Company learned to evoke the relaxation response. Five months later, they had less anxiety, high blood pressure and insomnia. They also found it easier to quit smoking, cut down on heavy drinking or lose weight. And they felt more assertive and happier.

Numerous studies confirm the profound effect meditation has on lowering blood pressure — and on lowering cholesterol levels — which makes it particularly beneficial to heart health. But deep relaxation remains its key benefit.

How the Relaxation Response Works

Unfortunately, although the stress response occurs automatically, Dr. Benson points out that the relaxation response must be "consciously and purposefully evoked." And lounging about on a La-Z-Boy recliner won't do it. To elicit the relaxation response you've got to get yourself into an altered state of consciousness.

That may sound mystical but, as Dr. Benson explains, an "altered state" merely refers to a level of consciousness that we don't ordinarily experience. If you've ever slipped into a trancelike state of wakefulness while gazing out a window or driving on a monotonous stretch of highway, you've already experienced altered consciousness. The relaxation response is evoked at another level, one that doesn't usually occur

Rx for Stress: Learn to Relax

When you include a set of relaxation techniques in your life, you're doing something very positive emotionally. You're focusing your attention on your own welfare—being unselfishly good to yourself. As Elliott F. Dacher, M.D., puts it, "People who learn to relax come out with a lot more than learning to relax. They develop an enhanced image of themselves, feel less helpless, more in control, capable of taking charge, of reversing disturbing facets of their lives."

And to people who say they don't have the time, Dr. Dacher rejoins, "What if you had a physical problem that required you to have bed rest twice a day in order to improve that condition? You'd do that, wouldn't you?"

spontaneously and that is described by researchers as a state of profound rest and heightened awareness.

Transcendental Meditation (TM) is one of the world's oldest and most scientifically documented techniques known to elicit this response. A revised and simplified form of yoga, it is the method on which most other meditation techniques are patterned. Unfortunately, TM is cloaked in a somewhat ritualistic $400-plus program. But for the cost of a book you can learn everything you need to know to practice a demystified version of TM—or one of several other effective relaxation techniques, including Progressive Relaxation and visualization. Although all these techniques are quite different in process, research tells us that they produce similar physiological changes.

Here, then is what to expect from TM and its alternatives, plus some practical advice to get you started on some common relaxation techniques.

Transcendental Meditation

TM has been around for more than 25 years, and as the granddaddy of relaxation techniques, it's the one most celebrated *and* criticized. Dr. Benson first discovered the relaxation response while studying people who practiced TM. And based on the number of TM-related research projects still under way, it appears the scientific fascination with this meditation method has not worn off. According to TM spokesperson Sam Katz, from the Maharishi International University in Washington, D.C., there are to date "over 350 scientific studies that show TM is beneficial." No other technique has anywhere near the same amount of scientific support.

Still, TM is a remarkably simple technique. Dr. Benson describes the process:

"A trained instructor gives you a secret word or sound or phrase, a mantra, which you promise not to divulge. This sound is allegedly chosen to suit the individual and is to be silently 'perceived.' The meditator receives the mantra from his teacher and then repeats it mentally over and over again while sitting in a comfortable position. Meditators are told to assume a passive attitude and if other thoughts come into mind to disregard them, going back to the mantra. Practitioners are advised to meditate 20 minutes in the morning, usually before breakfast, and 20 minutes in the evening, usually before dinner."

Learning the technique at any one of the 450 TM centers in the United States costs around $400 for a seven-lesson course. So for this one, you have to weigh that cost against the benefits: standard instruction by a qualified teacher and a huge body of scientific research that says TM works.

Dr. Benson's
Meditation-Relaxation Technique

Credit Dr. Herbert Benson with validating the benefits of meditation and removing some of the mystique. Thanks to him, and his best-selling book, *The Relaxation Response,* millions of people—from Main Street to Wall Street—now practice TM or a variation thereof. One of the most popular TM takeoffs is Dr. Benson's own method, which focuses on the very essence of meditation.

Like TM, Dr. Benson's technique for eliciting the relaxation response is best performed twice a day for 10 to 20 minutes, preferably before meals when you are less likely to fall asleep (dozing off may signal the onset of relaxation, but it curtails the full benefit of the relaxation response, Dr. Benson says). However, his technique allows for more individual flexibility. Whereas TM trainers would insist that two 20-minute meditation sessions each day are absolutely necessary for the success of the program, Dr. Benson suggests that, while that's the optimum, practicing the technique once a day for 20 minutes will have a favorable effect as well. Adherence to an inconvenient relaxation routine can create more tension than it helps to alleviate, he cautions. Now, for his technique:

1. Find a quiet environment free of distractions. A private room—away from telephones, street noise and other interruptions—is your best bet. If you need any paraphernalia to perform meditation, it may be a Do Not Disturb sign.

2. Choose a word or phrase—a mantra—to focus on. Dr. Benson recommends the word *one*. But you may prefer something else, like *love* or *peace*. It's nice if the word has special meaning to you, but it can be nonsensical, too, perhaps a sound or series of sounds that have a soothing tone. Once you pick your word, however, stick with it, says Dr. Benson. In time, then, you will come to associate that word with the calming effects of the relaxation response.

3. Sit upright in a comfortable position, with your hands resting naturally on your lap.

4. Let your eyes close gently and take a few moments to relax your muscles and quiet your mind. (Sometimes a few deep breaths help to prepare you for meditation.)

5. Now, breathing normally, become aware of each breath. Working with the slow, natural rhythm of your breathing, repeat your focus word or sound silently on every exhalation.

6. Disregard distractions; they're not important. "A passive attitude appears to be the most essential factor in eliciting the relaxation response," Dr. Benson points out. "Thoughts, imagery and feelings may drift into one's awareness. One should not concentrate on these perceptions but allow them to pass on."

7. Continue the exercise for 10 to 20 minutes. Use your judgment or sneak an occasional peek at a wristwatch to gauge

your time. Don't use a timer or alarm clock, as the noise can
be too disturbing. When your time is up, remain quiet for a
few minutes, with your eyes closed, to allow your thoughts to
readjust to full wakefulness.

Progressive Relaxation

About 70 years ago, a young graduate student from Harvard had a
profound insight: When we're under mental stress, we tense our
muscles; by tensing our muscles, we cause ourselves physical discomfort that tends to make our mental stress even worse. The student's
name name was Edmund Jacobson, and he went on to become a
renowned psychiatrist who gradually perfected a technique for breaking this tense-mind, tense-muscle cycle. He called it Progressive Relaxation.

Well, the technique has been enjoying something of a resurgence
lately. Psychologists and psychiatrists have been having luck treating
such stress-related disorders as headaches, ulcers, high blood pressure
and colitis with the technique (or adaptations of it).

How does it work? By forcing us to focus in on how it actually *feels*
to be physically relaxed.

Thomas D. Borkovec, Ph.D., a psychologist at Pennsylvania State
University who teaches relaxation courses, explains the process:

"We have the person start with the muscles of one hand, making a
fist, holding it for seven seconds, and then relaxing it," says Dr.
Borkovec. "Individuals soon learn to identify what both tension and
relaxation feel like, so that they will be able to detect tension throughout their bodies. After sufficient practice, most people are able to
deeply relax themselves within five minutes."

His students gradually learn to relax 16 of the body's muscle
groups, Dr. Borkovec says. They also inhale when they tense their
muscles, then exhale and relax very slowly (for about 45 seconds). That
is good therapy for people who also have trouble falling asleep, and its
effect improves with practice, Dr. Borkovec says.

Mastering the process.   To try the technique yourself, take
a comfortable position, either sitting in a chair with your hands resting
in your lap or lying down on your back with your feet against a wall or
heavy piece of furniture. Close your eyes.

Make a tight fist with your right hand, tensing the muscles in your wrist and forearm as you do. Hold tight for about five seconds, feeling the tension. Then unclench your fist, letting the tension drain from your forearm, wrist and fingers. Note the difference between how your arm feels now and how it felt when it was tense. Repeat.

Now allow your right forearm and hand to remain relaxed while you clench your left fist and tense your left forearm. Note the difference between how your left arm feels and how your relaxed arm feels. Now let your left arm relax, feeling the tension slowly drain out through your fingertips.

Next, tense your upper arms and shoulders. Hold a few seconds, the relax, again noting the difference between how your muscles feel when tense and how they feel when relaxed.

Now tense your neck. (It's probably the tensest part of your body.) Hold for a few seconds, then relax. At this point, your entire upper body should feel considerably more at ease than before you started.

Now make a frown, scowling as hard as you can. Relax. Try to feel the tension drain out of your eyes, cheeks and lips.

Raise up on your toes or, if you're lying down, push against the wall to create some tension in your legs. Hold for a few seconds, then relax. Again, try to notice the tension drain away. Now your entire body should feel more at peace.

Your breathing all the while should be normal and rhythmic. Upon conclusion, though, take a deep breath, feeling the tension in your chest. Exhale, breathe in again, hold, and let out, saying to yourself as you do, "I'm calm."

Repeat once or twice. Concentrate on how calm you are. Relish the sense of well-being throughout your entire body.

To conclude the exercise, slowly count to four. At one, you will begin to discard some of the deeper feelings of relaxation. At two, you are slightly more alert. At three, you will soon be ready to think and be fully alert. And at four, you may open your eyes.

Autogenic Training

Autogenic training is another natural and potent relaxation aid. This technique acts on the premise that your mind can compel your body to relax by concentrating on feelings of heaviness and warmth.

Through mental suggestion, the "heavy" muscles actually do relax, and the "warm" flesh receives better circulation, resulting in "a state of low physiological arousal," says Richard R. Bootzin, Ph.D., professor of psychology at Northwestern University.

In an experiment in 1968, researchers taught 16 college-student insomniacs to focus their attention on warmth and heaviness. At the end of the experiment, the students became so relaxed they were able to cut their average time needed to fall asleep from 52 to 22 minutes. These results matched the findings made by Dr. Bootzin in the Chicago area in 1974: "Daily practice of either Progressive Relaxation or autogenic training produced 50 percent improvement in time to fall asleep by the end of the one-month treatment period."

A Raggedy Ann doll, says psychologist Beata Jencks, Ph.D., is one image that can facilitate autogenic training. To feel heavy, she says, "make yourself comfortable and allow your eyes to close. Then lift one arm a little and let it drop. Let it drop heavily, as if it were the arm of one of those floppy dolls or animals. Choose one in your imagination. Choose a doll or an old, beloved, soft teddy bear." Once the mind fixes on the doll's image, Dr. Jencks says, lifting and dropping the arm in your imagination works as well as really letting it drop.

To invoke feelings of warmth, Dr. Jencks adds, "Imagine that you put your rag doll into the sun. Let it be warmed by the sun. You are the giant rag doll, and you are lying in the sun; all your limbs are nice and warm, but your head is lying in the shade and is comfortably cool."

Deep Breathing

Proper breathing, just by itself, is another way to reassure the autonomic nervous system that it can settle down and relax. That may sound simple enough, except for the fact that most of us have forgotten *how* to breathe properly.

Have you ever watched a baby breathe?

In and out, deep and even, slow and easy. As you watch, you can see how the baby's torso rises and falls with every breath. And if you look more closely, you will notice that it isn't the baby's chest that is going in and out, it's the tummy—or, more precisely, the diaphragm, the muscle between the chest and abdominal cavity, without which we couldn't breathe.

If you compare this to your own way of breathing, chances are you'll find it differs. If you're like most people, your upper chest expands as you inhale and contracts as you exhale. Over the years, you have learned to hold your stomach in.

This shift in breathing isn't a natural feature of growing older; many experts believe it is simply a bad habit. They also believe that by breaking the habit and returning to a style of breathing like that of an infant, we can help rid ourselves of chronic complaints such as headaches and fatigue. Not only that: By adopting proper breathing techniques, we may be able to ward off stress, lower our blood pressure, strengthen our hearts and more.

"The way we breathe has a profound effect on the way we feel," says psychologist Phil Nuernberger, Ph.D., author of *Freedom from Stress.* "Many stress-related complaints—whether physical, mental or emotional—are caused by improper breathing. But fortunately, many of these complaints can be reversed simply by learning to breathe properly."

In a series of studies conducted with more than 1,000 people in the last few years, James J. Lynch, Ph.D., of the Center for the Study of Human Psychophysiology at the University of Maryland School of Medicine in Baltimore, has found that you can help control your blood pressure with relaxation techniques, including proper breathing methods.

Dr. Lynch notes that many people tend to forget that one of the primary reasons our blood flows is in order to carry oxygen to our brain and vital organs. "If we don't take in enough oxygen by breathing, our blood has to circulate more rapidly to compensate and carry the same amount of oxygen. This can result in an increase in blood pressure, because our blood has to move faster to maintain the oxygen supply."

Our blood receives oxygen during a process called gas exchange, which takes place in our lungs. During gas exchange, oxygen is taken in by the blood while waste products, in the form of carbon dioxide, are released back into the lungs and exhaled.

"If you're breathing properly with the diaphragm, most of this gas exchange takes place in the lower part of the lungs," notes Alan Hymes, M.D., a cardiovascular surgeon and a member of the clinical faculty at the University of Minnesota School of Medicine in Minneapolis. Dr. Hymes is coauthor of the book *Science of Breath.* "Chest breathing will not reach the blood in the lower part of the lungs. It won't carry out this process as efficiently as diaphragmatic deep breathing will," he explains.

Studies conducted by Dr. Hymes and Dr. Nuernberger suggest that chest breathers may be more prone to heart attacks as well. In a survey of 153 heart attack patients at Methodist Hospital in Minneapolis, they found that all were primarily chest breathers.

Deep breathing decreases stress. One reason chest breathers may be more prone to heart attacks is that their bodies are under constant stress.

"Chest-type breathing may be directly related to activation of the flight-or-fight arousal system," explains Dr. Hymes. "In times of danger, when we need a burst of energy or strength in order to save our lives, this mechanism may be very helpful as it comes into play. However, when there is no need for this level of arousal, it may cause stress."

In his practice, Dr. Hymes has found that one way to alleviate this stress response is simply by consciously switching to a pattern of slow, deep, diaphragmatic breathing. "Try it the next time you find yourself becoming upset or angry," he suggests. "You'll be surprised at the change it makes in your perspective, and how calm your thinking becomes."

Diaphragmatic breathing also increases the production of endorphins, which are our bodies' own natural morphinelike painkilling substances. That's one reason why Donald Pentecost, M.D., a general practitioner in Fort Worth, Texas, prefers that his patients learn proper diaphragmatic breathing techniques.

"I have taught many of my patients how to breathe diaphragmatically," he says. "I have found it can be particularly helpful when patients are very uptight or disturbed. It works in a matter of minutes, helping to lower their blood pressure and heart rate and calming them down so they can talk more easily about what's bothering them."

Dr. Pentecost likes to teach his patients how to breathe diphragmatically before they undergo surgery. "Afterward, they are in too much pain and not as receptive. Yet I have found that if they learn the technique in advance and start breathing that way in the recovery room, they usually require less medication because they are in less pain postoperatively. They also experience fewer complications, such as pneumonia or splitting of sutures in gallbladder patients."

The technique is easy. Wearing loose clothes that do not restrict your midsection, assume a comfortable position either sitting in a chair or lying down. Keep your back as straight as possible.

Begin by breathing in slowly and evenly through your nostrils. In the first few sessions, keep your fingertips lightly on your abdomen and see how deep down into the abdomen you can breathe. Feel how your abdomen expands, then your rib cage, then your entire lungs.

To exhale, simply reverse the process, again breathing through your nostrils slowly and evenly. Finish the breath by gently contracting the abdomen and expelling the last of the stale air.

Don't strain. Never breathe beyond your capacity, trying to force air into your lungs. Just breathe rhythmically and easily, initially keeping your inhalation and exhalation the same length. Do this by using a slow mental count to three for the length of your inhalation and exhalation. As your breathing capacity improves, you can work slowly up to a higher count.

To make sure you're breathing diaphragmatically, Dr. Nuernberger suggests pretending that you are trying to blow up a balloon in your stomach. John Diamond, M.D., of Valley Cottage, New York, suggests that your mouth remain closed, with your tongue positioned on the roof of your mouth. "But don't clench your jaw," he warns.

Then exhale slowly. Most experts agree that it sometimes helps to exhale more slowly than we inhale. Dr. Nuernberger calls this "two-to-one" breathing, where the exhalation is twice as long as the inhalation. This type of breathing is a proven way of lowering stress in a hurry.

"Breathe through Your Fingertips"

The fine points of breathing have been described by Dr. Jencks in her book, *Your Body: Biofeedback at Its Best.*

"Imagine inhaling through your fingertips," Dr. Jencks writes, "up the arms, into the shoulders, and then exhaling down the trunk into the abdomen and legs, and leisurely out at the toes. Repeat, and feel how this slow, deep breathing affects the whole body, the abdomen, the flanks and the chest. Do not move the shoulders."

To inhale deeply, Dr. Jencks advises, pretend to inhale the fragrance of the first flower in spring, or imagine that your breathing rises and falls like ocean waves, or that the surface area of your lungs—if laid out flat—would cover a tennis court. That's how much air you can feel yourself breathing in.

Relief in a pinch.   Next time you're overwrought, notice how you're breathing. Chances are, if your juices are really flowing, your breathing is rapid and shallow. Slowing down your breathing is one of the quickest ways to reverse the effects of overstress, according to Jenny Steinmetz, Ph.D., a psychologist at the Kaiser Permanente Medical Center in Hayward, California.

"I tell my clients to slow their breathing to a seven-second inhale and an eight-second exhale," says Dr. Steinmetz, who is coauthor of *Managing Stress before It Manages You.* "Do four of those per minute for a total of two minutes and that discharges the stress immediately."

Using the second hand of a watch or clock is the easiest way to count the seconds, but if you don't have one nearby, Dr. Steinmetz has devised a clever alternative.

"All you have to do is say a number and then a three-syllable word to equal one second. For example, one el-e-phant, two el-e-phant, etc. I'll have people tell me that they've just had a 'ten-elephant' phone call or a 'six-elephant' lecture.

"The best thing about this method is that it can be done anywhere, any time, and you don't have to stop any other activity to do it. With enough practice it can actually become an 'automatic' type of response to stressful situations."

Visualization or Guided Imagery

If all else fails, use your imagination. That's the advice of physiologist Dr. Mary Asterita, who reminds us that stress, after all, isn't produced when certain events take place—it's the thinking and feeling, the imagining, about those events taking place that give you that gnawing, head-in-a-vise feeling. So it stands to reason that if our imagination can work *against* us, it can also be put to work *for* us, leading us to believe in the happiest outcome and eliciting the physiological relaxation response in the process.

Referred to as visualization or guided imagery, the technique involves simply playing out positive images in your mind. Visualize as many details—sights, sounds, smells and feelings—as you need to create a scene so real that your body becomes convinced it's happening.

The first thing you need to do, according to Dr. Asterita, is learn how to breathe deeply. Once you've gotten the hang of that, try this: "Right within yourself," says Dr. Asterita, "focus now on a rose. Now you're going to use all the senses. See the rose unfolding its soft petals. As you see it, notice the color; touch the rose and, in your mind's eye, feel the velvet texture. And as you feel it, enjoy the aromatic scent of this beautiful, unfolding rose. You see one color, but within that one color you see many shades. You are not only seeing the rose, you are *perceiving* it. You are *experiencing* it. Enjoy it for a few moments, and then slowly open your eyes." (You might want to tape-record yourself or someone with a soothing voice saying these instructions and those that follow, to be played back whenever you need to take a relaxation break. An instructive guiding voice is always a help.)

Sometimes in your imaginings, or visualizations, it helps to create a pressure atmosphere, a taut and tense and even unbearable situation, and then resolve it. By doing so in your mind, sometimes you can do the same in your real-life environment. For example, Dr. Asterita creates this scenario, which you should imagine with your eyes closed: "You're in a room and most of the people are smoking. The windows are closed, and it is so stuffy. You're sitting there, and you cannot move. You're far away from the door. And you are breathing in this smoke. See yourself there. Feel what it would be like if you were actually there. See the smoke. Experience it. See the people, everybody smoking and talking and anxious. A tense situation. And now, all of a sudden someone opens a window, and slowly you see the smoke leave, and fresh air enters the room. And now you can breathe clean fresh air. You take a nice deep breath, breathing in this vibrant, clean air. And now you become very comfortable and very relaxed."

Or perhaps you might want to try this one: "Imagine you're out camping in the woods and you're walking—but you have an overloaded backpack. It's heavy, and you really are feeling the weight. You don't want to carry this weight, and you can't walk carrying so much weight. As you're feeling this and thinking it, all of a sudden someone comes up next to you and begins to remove objects from the pack. Slowly, one by one, as they're removed, you're able to move freely and now breathe more deeply. And now you enjoy taking some nice deep breaths, breathing in deeply as you feel a sense of weight being lifted."

You can create your own tense situations and then provide the welcome relief or the knight in shining armor coming to the rescue. Search your psyche for the dreads hiding there and for the devices that will remove them. If you work it right, it should make you feel a whole lot better—without drugs, without added expense, without packing up your troubles and moving to a deserted island in the South Pacific.

Massage

Want to try your own brand of "therapeutic touch"—to ease tense muscles, get your blood flowing freely, move into a relaxed state and generally feel good? Then give massage a try.

Swedish massage is the best-known type. It's your basic rubbing, stroking, kneading, tapping kind of massage that leaves you feeling peaceful and tingly all over. Shiatsu is a Japanese massage that uses thumb and finger pressure. This pressure is applied to various points of the body, each designed to affect a different set of muscle systems. There are several shiatsu massage forms, each for a specific purpose— for instance, one makes you feel serene, another makes you more energetic, a third increases sexual vigor, and yet another helps get rid of aches and pains.

How do you find a good masseur or masseuse? The best way is to get a friend's enthusiastic recommendation, or try your local physical therapist for a recommendation.

If you decide on a home massage, try the buddy system. Take turns with a friend giving and receiving a massage. This is all you'll need: a willing partner, your hands, some oil and a couple of towels spread on the floor. (A bed isn't a good place for a massage. No matter how firm the mattress, there's not enough support.) Choose a comfortably warm room, avoiding chills and drafts. Begin by applying baby oil or vegetable oil to your hands to avoid friction during the massage.

When experimenting on your own, try a back or neck rub—areas of the body where tension so often settles. For a back rub, straddle your partner's thighs. Be careful not to rest your weight *on* your partner, otherwise she or he will tense up. Rub your hands briskly together to spread the oil and warm your hands. Place your hands on your partner's lower back, one to the left of the spine, the other to the right, and apply pressure firmly up along each side. When you get to the neck, brush your hands lightly along the spine until you get back to the base of the spine. Next, working slowly and as close to the spine as possible, use your thumbs to make short, firm strokes up along both sides of the spine. When you reach the neck, gently knead the muscles that curve from the neck to the shoulders between your fingers and thumbs.

As you work through the various steps, keep your hands relaxed. Don't assume positions that tense you up, because you'll communicate that tension to your partner. Ask for, and be responsive to, feedback. The pressure you exert should come mainly from the weight of your body, not your hands or arms. Feel for knots, tight muscles and tender spots, and give those more attention.

Biofeedback

Biofeedback is a technique that helps you learn about and gain control of those secret inner workings of your body. Using a machine that gives you instant feedback (hence the name), you can learn to recognize and then duplicate desirable body states, such as having low blood pressure or feeling relaxed. Complete success means weaning yourself off the machine after learning how to control these physical mechanisms.

Because biofeedback training can be a relatively expensive relaxation approach—especially in contrast to those that don't cost a cent—we'll give you both the pros and the cons in detail.

High drama accompanied biofeedback's entry into the world in the early 1960s. Hordes of medical writers and some psychologists pounced: Here, they seemed to say, was a miracle cure, electronics come to alleviate our pain and suffering. Predictably, it couldn't live up to inflated expectations, and in some scientific circles it has been relegated to the status of an expensive toy. As is so often the case, the truth falls somewhere between the extremes. A fair number of people use biofeedback, some in laboratory training sessions, others at home.

Although it is no cure-all, biofeedback nevertheless can help some people. Are you often tense and headachy? Through biofeedback you may learn to unstress yourself. Do you grind your teeth, either when you are awake and thinking nervous thoughts or when you're asleep and having nervous dreams? Through biofeedback you may learn to stop this stress-related habit, which can create serious dental and jaw muscle problems. Do you unconsciously clench your jaw muscles when you're feeling tense? Through biofeedback you may learn to abandon this automatic clenching, a bad habit that can bring on headaches and neck pain and throw your teeth out of alignment.

Biofeedback has helped people suffering from a variety of disorders. An example is Raynaud's disease, a circulatory disorder in which either emotional stress or exposure to cold constricts the blood vessels in the extremities, causing fingers or toes to turn icy and blue. Some people learn to warm their extremities through biofeedback. And biofeedback has controlled another circulation problem—high blood pressure.

Chandra Patel, M.D., of the London School of Hygiene and Tropical Medicine in England, headed a team of researchers working with a large group of people with high blood pressure. These people were offered a smorgasbord of relaxation techniques—breathing exercises, deep muscle relaxation and meditation—along with biofeedback training. Another group of hypertensives received only counseling and lectures. After two months, the members of the biofeedback training group had a greater reduction in blood pressure than those in the group that didn't get the training. They were also smoking less and their cholesterol levels were lower.

As that British study suggests, you don't just hook yourself up to a machine and start relaxing. What you do is hook up, practice breathing or one of the other techniques, and instantly get a signal that tells you how you are doing. Explains Jeffrey Rudolph, Psy.D., director of the Multimodal Therapy Institute in New York City, "The machine is not therapy. It's not an end but a means to an end. You get feedback—objective data. The machine also facilitates motivation and learning."

How it works.   Let's take a look at a typical session of biofeedback. You have a chronic headache (or neck ache, or lower back pain)—muscle tension pain. The specialist takes your stress history, tries to get a sense of when the pain comes and goes, then hooks you up to an electromyograph (EMG). Specifically, he places electrodes, held down by tape or an adjustable band, on the skin close to your forehead or the back of your neck. (That's for headache; other spots are used for other kinds of muscle tension.) Wires run from the electrodes to the EMG, where electronic wizardry takes place: The machine converts bioelectrical charges from the muscles into a biofeedback signal you can hear as a sound that varies in pitch, or as a series of clicks that go faster or slower, depending on how stressed you feel or how well you're able to relax. Thus, you immediately become aware of your body's stress reactions and the power you have to diminish or intensify them. You also can readily discover which kind of relaxation technique works best for you.

Another commonly used instrument is the temperature trainer, which reads minute temperature changes in the body, translating them into signals you can hear or see. A sensor slips over a finger, and wires run to the machine. It teaches you to control the temperature of various parts of your body, especially your hands. "It's used for all disorders relating to the heart and circulatory system," Dr. Rudolph says, and for migraine headaches. At least some people who suffer from migraines say they get cold hands prior to the onset of a migraine attack, and there are reports of migraine sufferers being helped by finger-warming biofeedback training.

The process becomes more understandable when you consider that tiny muscles surround your blood vessels. Relaxed muscles allow for a heavier blood flow and thus more heat. Constricted muscles reduce the flow, thus reducing heat. By learning to control these muscles—once thought to be involuntary—we can relax and warm up.

A third instrument you see in use a lot is the Galvanic Skin Response (GSR). Like the lie detector, it measures sweat gland activity through the electrical conductivity of the skin. The more activity, the more stress you're under. Again, you get instant auditory or visual feedback to let you know how you're doing. Like the EMG, the GSR can be used as a general stress monitor, showing you the level of stress you're under and helping you to retrain to lower levels.

Biofeedback is not for everyone. These specific biofeedback machines are only some of the variations on this theme. Would one of them help you? It depends.

Biofeedback is not for you, for example, if you're in the small minority whose stress levels aren't picked up by the machines. This technique also is not for you if you start out being strongly skeptical, if you're easily frustrated, or if you're going to become so dependent on it that you'll take your stress readings ten times a day. "People who take continuous readings keep resensitizing instead of desensitizing themselves to stress," Dr. Rudolph explains.

You absolutely also need stick-to-itiveness. Many people do a beautiful job of relaxing in the laboratory, but once they're finished with the formal training they put their newfound relaxation skills into the closet, never to look at them again. Or they buy an expensive machine and after a few tries put *it* into that closet, never to look at it again. Persistence is very important. On the other hand, if you have

On-the-Job Stress Control

Busy schedules, approaching deadlines, high-pressured competition and even problems outside of the working environment are all causes of stress. But today some of our nation's companies are offering their employees programs in meditation, relaxation and other forms of stress management. Even Ma Bell meditates.

In fact, the New York Telephone Company (NYT) was a pioneer in the field of employee meditation programs. In 1978 Patricia Carrington, Ph.D., and a team of researchers from the department of psychology at Princeton University began a study of stress reduction, using 154 NYT employees as guinea pigs. These employees were all self-identified as being under a great deal of stress.

At the onset of the study the employees were divided into four groups. Two learned to practice meditation techniques — Clinically Standardized Meditation and Respiratory One Method Meditation. Both are forms of meditation in which a selected sound is verbally or mentally repeated to achieve a calming persistence, enjoy gadgetry and learn well when you get instant feedback, biofeedback training may work for you.

Do-it-yourself vs. professional training.   If you decide to try biofeedback, should you go to a professional or buy a home-use machine? The professionals say that one-to-one training, with extensive laboratory work and home assignments, does the better job. That's probably true, but finances can be a consideration. Working with a professional biofeedback trainer may involve 12 or more sessions, costing as much as $75 a session. A good home-use machine runs about $100. Some biofeedback enthusiasts do both—go to a profes-

effect. The third group was taught Progressive Relaxation, a muscle-relaxing technique. And the fourth served as a "waiting list" control group.

At the end of six months the results were amazing. All of the groups showed a marked reduction in stress; even the symptoms of the control group decreased, leading researchers to believe that a placebo effect had occurred. When tested for individual symptoms, the participants were less depressed, anxious, hostile, psychotic, paranoid and compulsive.

The meditating groups showed the most improvement, however. Many of the volunteers in these two groups said that they were able to think, remember and organize their thoughts better. They felt that they had a better handle on life's problems. They were even getting more enjoyment out of life. A more satisfied bunch of guinea pigs would be hard to find.

NYT, pleased with the study, continued the program and expanded it to include eight of their branch offices. They believe—and it has been proven true—that happy employees lead to a happier and more productive company.

sional and get their own instrument. Either way, the trick is to learn those relaxation techniques that work best for you, and learn them so well that in time they'll be part of your daily life and you'll no longer need a machine, either at home or in somebody's lab.

Build Stress Control into Your Life

From laughter to stretching and boogie to biofeedback—the ways to reduce stress in your life are very different, but also very effective. You may want to use some of them—or even all of them—to help you cope.

First, you might begin by scheduling time into your busy day for your antistress activities. Perhaps playing tapes of your favorite music as you commute to work, either in your car or—if you are a passenger and *only* if you are a passenger—directly into your ears. Make appointments for your biofeedback or yoga classes. And remember, too, that just plain old exercise also helps you to release stress. Plan for some vigorous activity such as a brisk walk or a long swim three or more times a week. (Perhaps competitive games should be shelved during periods of tension, since even winning can generate a certain level of stress.)

Along with all this activity, remember also to be *in*active. Set up a time of day, every day—perhaps right before dinner—when you unplug the phone, close the bedroom door, turn off the light and sit, meditating quietly.

In addition to these techniques, it is important to remember that you have control over the stress in your life. You can work at destressing yourself the same way you can work at losing weight, building muscle or even weeding the garden. The secret rests in taking action. Inaction leads to becoming the victim of stressful circumstances. Applying common sense and stress-coping techniques leads to a winning attitude and a brighter life.

How Music Soothes the Soul

You settle back in your easy chair with your feet up and a pillow behind you. On the turntable is Pachelbel's *Canon in D Major.* As the celestial music fills the room, your body relaxes and your mind unwinds. The music holds you and lifts you, carries you beside beautiful wooded brooks and through cities of gold.

Physiologically, your heartbeat and breathing are both slowing down and becoming more regular, synchronizing themselves with the beat of the music. Your airways are opening up. Your blood pressure probably drops a few points to a more serene level.

The resplendent strains of Baroque music have a direct impact on your autonomic nervous system. Your heart, your smooth muscles (like your stomach), your gland system, even your metabolic rate, all respond.

Pitch, harmonics, tempo, melody—all contribute to the effect music will have on your mind and body. But the most important factor, says composer and researcher Steven Halpern, Ph.D., is your individual response.

Tempos of around 50 to 60 beats per minute are usually the most soothing. Some researchers theorize that this tempo's calming effect may result from its similarity to our mother's heartbeat, which we heard in the womb.

Psychiatrists, who have successfully used music in place of sedatives and other drugs to reach and relax people with deep emotional disturbances, also point out that music touches us at our most fundamental level of feeling.

But how can we choose the music that will have the most calming effect on us? Simple, says Dr. Halpern. Just check your breathing. if it is deepening and becoming more regular, the music is relaxing you.

C H A P T E R
F O U R T E E N

The Calming Power of Prayer

Regular church attendance provides a sense of community, long-term friendships and a feeling of security in the rapidly changing and fast-paced world. It can even lower blood pressure!

According to Gene Stainbrook, Ph.D., M.P.H., from the Center for Health Promotion, Research and Development at the University of Texas, regular attendance at a church, synagogue or other place of worship has many physical and emotional benefits. "Regular attendance gives people social support, a sense of fellowship and common goals," says Dr. Stainbrook.

He also suggests that church gives people a moral and ethical framework that helps them handle everyday stress. And attending church provides many community service opportunities. "There are indications that helping others makes you happier and healthier," reports Dr. Stainbrook.

A study done at Bowling Green State University in Ohio supports these theories. Researchers studied what is perhaps life's most stressful situation—the "twin processes" of immigration and assimilation into a new culture. They found that new citizens who had a religious association experienced a fuller sense of community *and* had lower blood pressure than did their nonattending counterparts. And church-going newcomers were also more likely to become U.S. citizens.

The ritual itself is another important aspect of any religious service. Both passive and active types of rituals have organizing and calming effects on church-goers. "Some people want a lot of active involvement in their religious service, others want quiet and meditation — both are beneficial," says Dr. Stainbrook. "What you choose just depends on which you prefer."

Dial H-E-L-P

Where did you turn the last time you had a problem — a problem so serious or so personal that you chose not to discuss it with a friend, a relative or your family doctor? Maybe you reached out for your telephone — and a counselor manning the hotline at the other end.

If so, you made a wise move. Hotlines are available for almost every problem. They are found all across the country and some are open around the clock to help you in a time of crisis. And studies have shown these hotlines to be highly effective. In fact, one study reported that more than 90 percent of those who called a hotline were satisfied.

Much of this success can be attributed to those standing by the phones. While some counselors are professionals, others are simply caring people who have been trained to deal effectively with the problems they encounter.

Yet the hotlines are not without their problems. Because many callers remain anonymous, they cannot be reached for follow-up counseling.

Despite these difficulties, hotlines offer several real advantages.

Many are free. All offer the opportunity to remain anonymous. And, perhaps most important, they bring the comforting realization that there is always someone available to lend an ear, just when you need it most.

Abused and Battered Adults
Battered Women Hotline
24 hours, 7 days
Cleveland, Ohio: (216) 961-4422

Victims' Service Hotline
24 hours, 7 days
New York City: (212) 577-7777

Abused and Battered Children
Child Abuse
Florida only: (800) 342-9152

Child Abuse
New York City only: (800) 342-3720

Child Abuse Careline
Connecticut only: (800) 842-2288

Child Abuse Hotline
24 hours, 7 days
Missouri only: (800) 392-3738

Childline
24 hours, 7 days
Pennsylvania only: (800) 932-0313

Family Crisis Center
24 hours, 7 days
Denver, Colo.: (303) 893-6111

Massachusetts Society for the
  Prevention of Cruelty to Children
  (M.S.P.C.C.)
9:00 A.M.-5:00 P.M., weekdays
  (no holidays)
Boston, Mass.: (617) 227-2280

National Child Abuse Center
Denver, Colo.: (303) 231-3963

Parents Anonymous
24 hours (daytime preferred), 7 days
Nationwide: (800) 421-0353
California only: (800) 352-0386

Age-Related Problems
Elderly Hotline
8:00 A.M.-5:00 P.M., weekdays
Boston, Mass.: (617) 722-4646

Senior Citizens of Greater Dallas
8:00 A.M.-5:00 P.M., weekdays
Dallas, Tex.: (214) 823-5700

Seniors' Resource Center
8:00 A.M.-5:00 P.M., weekdays
  (no holidays)
Wheat Ridge, Colo.: (303) 238-8151

Agoraphobia
The Agoraphobia and Anxiety Center
  of Temple University
9:00 A.M.-5:00 P.M., weekdays
Bala Cynwyd, Pa.: (215) 667-6490

Territorial Apprehensiveness (TERRAP)
9:00 A.M.-5:00 P.M., weekdays
Menlo Park, Calif.:
(415) 327-1312; (415) 329-1233

Alcoholism
Al-Anon
(Help for the families and friends of
  alcoholics.)
8:00 A.M.-5:00 P.M., weekdays
Worldwide: (212) 302-7240
10:00 A.M.-3:00 P.M., Monday and
  Friday only
Southern New Jersey only:
  (609) 547-0855

Alcohol 24-Hour Help Line
7 days
Eastern and Midwestern states:
  (800) 252-6465
West of the Rockies: (800) ALCOHOL

Alcoholics Anonymous
(Offers information about AA chapters
  nationwide.)
9:00 A.M.-4:30 P.M., weekdays
New York City: (212) 686-1100

Breastfeeding
La Leche League International, Inc.
8:00 A.M.-3:00 P.M., weekdays
Franklin Park, Ill.: (312) 455-7730

Cancer
National Cancer Institute
7:00 A.M.-midnight, 7 days
Nationwide: (800) 638-6694

Counseling
CONTACT Teleministries
24 hours, 7 days
Harrisburg, Pa.: (717) 232-3501

Women in Transition
24 hours, 7 days
Philadelphia, Pa.: (215) 922-7500

Crime Victims and Witnesses
Victim Hotline
24 hours, 7 days
Manhattan, N.Y.: (212) 577-7777

Crisis Intervention
Crisis Center
24 hours, 7 days
Detroit, Mich.: (313) 224-7000

Crisis Clinic
24 hours, 7 days
Seattle, Wash.: (206) 447-3222

Crisis Line
24 hours, 7 days
Miami, Fla.: (305) 358-4357

Women Organized Against Rape
24 hours, 7 days
Philadelphia, Pa.: (215) 922-3434

Drug Abuse
Phoenix House
24 hours, 7 days
California: (714) 953-9373

Drug Side Effects
Office of Drug Information
8:00 A.M.-4:30 P.M., weekdays
Rockville, Md.: (301) 295-8012

Eating Disorders
American Anorexia-Bulimia
    Association, Inc.
9:00 A.M.-5:00 P.M., weekdays
Teaneck, N.J.: (201) 836-1800

National Association of Anorexia
    Nervosa and Associated Disorders,
    Inc.
9:00 A.M.-5:00 P.M., weekdays
Highland Park, Ill.: (312) 831-3438

Overeaters Anonymous
Worldwide: (215) 848-3191

Gambling Abuse
Debtors Anonymous
9:00 A.M.-5:00 P.M., weekdays
New York City: (212) 484-2555

Gamblers Anonymous
9:00 A.M.-5:00 P.M., weekdays
Los Angeles, Calif.: (213) 386-8789

Marital Problems
Divorce-Anonymous
9:00 A.M.-5:00 P.M., 6 days
Chicago, Ill.: (312) 341-9843

Poison Emergencies
Seattle Poison Center
(Gives emergency advice across the
    country, but check for the regional
    center nearest you.)
24 hours, 7 days
Seattle, Wash.: (206) 526-2121

Pregnancy
Birthright
9:30 A.M.-12:30 P.M., Monday-Friday;
7:00 P.M.-9:00 P.M., Monday-Thursday
Woodbury, N.J.: (609) 848-1818

National Pregnancy Hotline
24 hours, 7 days
Nationwide: (800) 238-4269
8:00 A.M.-5:00 P.M., weekdays
California only: (800) 233-6058

Rape
(*See also* Crisis Intervention)
Rape Help Line
(Listed in most cities as Rape Crisis
    Center.)
24 hours, 7 days
New York City: (212) 777-4000

Runaways
National Runaway Switchboard
24 hours, 7 days
Nationwide: (800) 621-4000

Runaway Hotline
24 hours, 7 days
Nationwide: (800) 231-6946

Single Parents
Parents without Partners
9:00 A.M.-5:00 P.M., weekdays
Washington, D.C.: (301) 588-9354

Smoking
Action on Smoking and Health
  (ASH)
9:00 A.M.-4:00 P.M., weekdays
Washington, D.C.: (202) 659-4310

Office on Smoking and Health
8:00 A.M.-4:30 P.M., weekdays
Rockville, Md.: (301) 443-1575

Suicide
Suicide and Crisis Intervention Center
24 hours, 7 days
Philadelphia, Pa.: (215) 686-4420

The Samaritans
(Will refer to help sources throughout
  the country.)
24 hours, 7 days
New York City: (212) 673-3000
Boston, Mass.: (617) 247-0220

Surgery
National Second Surgical Opinion
  Program Hotline
8:00 A.M.-midnight, 7 days
Nationwide: (800) 638-6833
Maryland only: (800) 492-6603

Unwanted Pregnancy
National Abortion Federation Hotline
9:30 A.M.-5:30 P.M., weekdays
Nationwide: (800) 772-9100

Venereal Disease
National VD Hotline
Nationwide: (800) 227-8922

Operation Venus
9:00 A.M.-9:00 P.M., weekdays
Pennsylvania only: (800) 462-4966